DOGFIGHT 7

F-8 Crusader
Vietnam 1963–73

Peter E. Davies

OSPREY PUBLISHING
Bloomsbury Publishing Plc
Kemp House, Chawley Park, Cumnor Hill, Oxford,
OX2 9PH, UK
29 Earlsfort Terrace, Dublin 2, Ireland
1385 Broadway, 5th Floor, New York, NY 10018, USA
E-mail; info@ospreypublishing.com
www.ospreypublishing.com

OSPREY is a trademark of Osprey Publishing Ltd

First published in Great Britain in 2023

A catalogue record for this book is available from the British
Library.

ISBN: PB 9781472857545; eBook 9781472857521;
ePDF 9781472857538; XML 9781472857552

23 24 25 26 27 10 9 8 7 6 5 4 3 2 1

Edited by Tony Holmes
Cover and battlescene artwork by Gareth Hector
Ribbon and tactical diagrams by Tim Brown
Armament artworks by Jim Laurier
Maps by www.bounford.com
Index by Fionbar Lyons
Typeset by PDQ Digital Media Solutions, UK
Printed and bound in India by Replika Press Private Ltd.

Osprey Publishing supports the Woodland Trust, the UK's
leading woodland conservation charity.

To find out more about our authors and books visit www.
ospreypublishing.com. Here you will find extracts, author
interviews, details of forthcoming events and the option to sign
up for our newsletter.

Front Cover Artwork: VF-162 CO Cdr Dick Bellinger (in
F-8E Crusader BuNo 149159), whose unit was part of
CVW-16 embarked in *Oriskany*, and his wingman, Lt Lee
Prost, were a TARCAP section for an October 9, 1966 A-4
Skyhawk strike on the Phu Ly bridge south of Hanoi. They
were orbiting at very low altitude when the offshore radar
controller PIRAZ ship reported two MiG-21s approaching at
higher altitude ahead of them. With a second TARCAP section,
they climbed to engage as one MiG dived to attack an *Iron
Hand* anti-missile A-4.

Bellinger approached within 1.5 miles of the trailing
MiG-21PFL of the VPAF's 921st Fighter Regiment, this aircraft
being flown by Nguyen Van Minh. Minh saw the Crusaders
and flew a "split-S" maneuver, inverting his aircraft and turning
beneath Bellinger's F-8E. Bellinger dived inverted, and as his
nose passed a 20-degree angle he fired single AIM-9B and
AIM-9D Sidewinders in quick succession, hitting the MiG with
both missiles. Minh ejected and Bellinger continued a
high-speed dive at 60 degrees before just about managing to roll
his aircraft level and pull out very close to the ground. The
MiG crashed into a paddy field. Bellinger had claimed the US
Navy's first MiG-21 kill, and he was awarded a Silver Star for
his success. (Cover artwork by Gareth Hector)

Previous Page: Two F-8Es from VF-211 prepare to launch
from *Bon Homme Richard*'s port catapult while a pair of F-8Cs
from VF-24 line up for a starboard cat shot. NP 448
(foreground) was Lt(jg) Philip Dempewolf's "Page Boy 448" on
July 21, 1967 during a major dogfight in which he scored a
probable MiG-17 victory, while two more fell to Lt Cdrs Bob
Kirkwood and "Tim" Hubbard from CVW-21. (US Navy)

Acknowledgments – Sincere thanks are due to Kev Darling,
Capt Jerry B. Houston US Navy (ret), Cdr Vern Larson US
Navy (ret), Cdr Peter B. Mersky US Navy (ret), Terry Panopalis,
Cdr Alex Rucker US Navy (ret), Capt Richard W. Schaffert US
Navy (ret), and Lt Phil Vampatella US Navy (ret).

DOGFIGHT

Contents

CHAPTER 1
IN BATTLE

When the US Navy entered the Vietnam conflict it had an aircraft which was often described as the only true air superiority fighter of its time. The powerful, maneuverable Mach 1.6-capable F-8 Crusader, described by MiG killer Lt Phil Wood as a "macho fighter pilot's dream," was the weapon of Naval Aviators who achieved an unprecedented four aerial victories against MiG-21s without loss and 14 kills against MiG-17s for only three losses. To achieve this in a fighter which had the highest operational loss rate of any US tactical aircraft of its day, as well as armament that was often unreliable, was a tribute to the Crusader pilots' dedication to the art of dogfighting in an era in which many air forces considered such tactics outmoded and irrelevant.

In Vietnam, the confrontations between Seventh Fleet Crusaders and MiGs of the Vietnamese Peoples' Air Force (VPAF) were rare. Indeed, many pilots would routinely complete two combat tours without seeing an enemy aircraft. However, those that did encounter communist MiG-17s or MiG-21s usually became embroiled in some of the most intense dogfights of the war involving numerous demonstrations of the skill, ingenuity, and courage of the Crusader pilots.

There is no better example of this than the extended ten-minute dogfight that took place on December 14, 1967 between Lt Cdr Richard W. Schaffert of VF-111 (embarked in USS *Oriskany* (CVA-34)) and four MiG-17s that were attempting to engage an *Iron Hand* A-4 Skyhawk pilot who had been tasked with attacking surface-to-air missile (SAM) sites near Haiphong. A US Navy fighter pilot since 1956, the highly experienced Schaffert was flying his 276th mission over North Vietnam when he fought the quartet of VPAF MiGs in F-8C BuNo 146999, which was armed with three AIM-9D Sidewinders. His Crusader used the same "Pouncer" call-sign as the *Iron Hand* A-4Es involved in the SAM suppression mission. As Schaffert subsequently recalled:

We went "feet dry" over the mouth of the Red River and "straight up the gut" for the Canal des Bambous. Our mission was to mine that heavily transited waterway with Mk 36 Destructor fused weapons before the Christmas bombing halt. We were part of a flight of nine A-4E mine layers with two F-8E TARCAP [Target Combat Air Patrol – the latter provided by VF-162 skipper Cdr Cal Swanson and Lt Dick Wyman] and two pairs of A-4E/F-8C *Iron Hand* SAM suppressors. My VF-111 skipper, [Cdr] Bob Rasmussen, was escorting VA-164's [Lt] Denny Weichmann and I was escorting their capable Shrike-shooter, [Lt(jg)] Chuck Nelson. After going "feet dry," the TARCAP accelerated ahead and we *Iron Handers* moved away on either side of the formation to search for SAM sites.

We were approaching the middle of the Red River delta when "Red Crown" [the call-sign for the fighter controller embarked in a radar-equipped US Navy warship offshore] broadcast "Four 'red bandits' [MiG-17s] airborne from 'Bullseye' [Gia Lam airfield in Hanoi] heading east." I was envious of the TARCAP, and became even more so when the next transmission was to our strike group, telling them that the "red bandits" were on their nose at a range of 30km and closing. The calls kept coming as the MiGs apparently closed with their intended targets, and the crackling in my headset warned me of a SAM guidance radar ["Fan Song"] locking onto us.

When "Red Crown" called "'Red bandits,' bearing 270 degrees at two miles," I was inverted at 18,000ft and 350kts, heading west, about 3,000ft abeam on the right side of Chuck's A-4E. I tried to focus my eyes into the setting sun and saw the reflection of a windscreen at "12 o'clock," slightly down and less than a mile away – two MiG-17s in fighting wing formation. As they passed underneath Chuck, I called "Tally Ho" and then pulled my nose down hard and left into the MiGs. It occurred to me that "Red Crown" had probably mistaken Chuck and me for the main strike group.

The MiG section began a nose-high left turn back towards Chuck. I went into afterburner to boost my speed. The MiG section was about a mile north, up 3,000ft and continuing their left climbing turn. I completed my left diving turn with 45 degrees angle off the wingman's tail and pulled my nose up to attack. The MiG-17 was in my gunsight and I had a good Sidewinder tone in my earphones. I fired the AIM-9D at a range of about 5,000ft and with 45 degrees angle-off. The MiG leader broke hard to the left and his wingman was thrown to the outside of the turn. My Sidewinder passed under the wingman's starboard wing without fusing.

When I looked back over my shoulder for Chuck, I saw another section of MiG-17s coming out of the sun 3,000ft away. The nose of the lead MiG lit up as he began firing. I instinctively snapped my F-8C's G-forces from 4.5 to 8g. Tracers passed low and behind. Both MiGs overshot and flew outside my turn radius. I relaxed some G-force on my Crusader and continued a vertical climb in afterburner, feeling the need to get on top of the fight to see what was down there! I called Chuck, "'Pouncer Three,' 'Pouncer Four.' Lost sight of you. There's at least four of them. Get the hell out of here!" He calmly replied "I'm locked on a 'Fan Song' and commencing an attack." That gutsy Shrike-shooter was doing his job, and I had to do mine!

VF-111's Lt Cdr Dick Schaffert poses beside an F-8C on board *Oriskany* in 1967–68 during the vessel's brutal third war cruise that saw CVW-16 lose 29 aircraft in combat and ten more to operational accidents – 20 aircrew were killed and seven captured. (US Navy)

Bui Van Suu (in "Red 2037") and Le Hai from the 923rd FR release the brakes in their Shenyang J-5s (Chinese-built MiG-17Fs) and commence a formation take-off from Gia Lam on December 17, 1967. (István Toperczer Collection)

The MiG section that I attacked had rejoined and was about 10,000ft directly below me, diving for airspeed in a left turn. A second MiG section was coming up, but they wouldn't have enough energy to reach me. I decided on another attack upon the lower, first section, rolling inverted and pulling my nose down. My plan was to meet the climbing second section head-on as I dived on the first section. Unfortunately, the wingman [in the second section] remained in close fighting wing formation. I flew through a dangerous hail of tracers from both MiGs as we passed nose-to-nose. The first section, meanwhile, was continuing its defensive spiral.

To counter the MiG-17s' superior turning ability I performed a barrel roll to the outside of their turning circle, then followed with a second roll to reduce the angle off their tail. When I was finally within a 45-degree cone of the tailpipe of the MiG leader, he was slightly nose down and my Sidewinder's field of vision included reflections of the setting sun off the paddy fields below.

I fired my second AIM-9D with a good tone. The missile came off the rail and headed for the lead MiG. My attention was then immediately distracted by tracers blazing over my canopy. I jammed the stick forward and kicked full left rudder in a negative-G roll underneath and stayed in a vertical dive for airspeed. The attacking second section of MiGs broke off their gunnery run with a barrel roll away, and then followed me down in the dive, about 5,000ft behind. To avoid cannon fire if the MiGs cut me off in my pull-out [from the dive], I waited until the last nano-second before bringing the stick firmly back in a 7g pull-out. I saw the red roof of a pagoda to my right, less than 200ft away. I kept the high-G on until I was again in a vertical climb, then engaged the afterburner. The MiGs had pulled out of their dive at around 3,000ft. I flashed past them vertically and zoomed to 25,000ft. I waited while they tried vainly to soar up, but both jets "fell off" below.

I then looked west for Chuck's A-4E and saw two MiG-21s coming out of the sun. I hit the afterburner and began an accelerating turn into them. At almost 90 degrees and 4,000ft away, they each fired two missiles. All four missiles maintained steady flight towards the east without any indication of tracking me. The MiG-21s continued east, out of the fight. Perhaps their missile-firing distracted the MiG-17 section that was climbing towards me, for they leveled off 10,000ft below me and began a turn to the east.

I initiated a barrel roll attack from about 1.5 miles behind them, approaching their altitude when the leader saw me and broke hard left. The maneuver threw his wingman out of the turn. I had a clear Sidewinder tone on him from about 6,000ft and 40 degrees angle-off. I fired my third and last missile, then I immediately followed with an outside barrel roll to position myself behind the leader. I was

about 3,000ft behind with 150 knots of closing speed, tracking smoothly. I began firing 20mm at 2,000ft range with the first tracers flying on a line directly behind and approaching the MiG-17. He went into a maximum-G turn; the planform of his aircraft changed. I went to 6.5g to maintain tracking but my guns jammed before the line of tracers reached the MiG!

I rocked my wings level and snapped my nose up to clear the target. The MiG reversed quickly and sprayed the area below and behind me with tracers. I stayed in afterburner, went into a vertical climb and quickly pulled out of range. I continued my climb until almost out of airspeed and did a zero angle-of-attack rudder reversal to fall straight down on the MiG. I then avoided a turning fight by forcing the MiG leader into a series of rolling scissors maneuvers. The superior engine thrust of my Crusader offset the high lift of the MiG's superior wing. We locked in a continual roll, canopy to canopy, first diving then climbing in the vertical plane. Separation between the aircraft diminished with each scissors maneuver. After six gut-wrenching maneuvers, I was distracted by a "low fuel" warning light and had no choice but to disengage. At the bottom of the next scissors I simply rolled away from the MiG and accelerated to the east at treetop height. I was already a mile ahead when the MiG turned back.

It was a long run from going "feet wet" [over the sea] to *Oriskany*. There were no tankers available. As I stared at that rapidly dropping fuel gauge it seemed to get bigger and bigger. Would it end up bringing me down when I had just out-fought six MiGs? To occupy my adrenalin-soaked mind I recorded the major points of the fight on my kneeboard in the shorthand I had developed for more than 500 air combat training flights I had instructed during five years at Advanced Training and Replacement Air Wing squadrons. Thankfully, *Oriskany* was on a recovery course to the east and I was cleared for a straight-in approach. I caught the No. 3 arresting wire with two minutes of fuel remaining.

Dick Schaffert was awarded the Distinguished Flying Cross for his outstanding flying during this engagement.

VF-111 F-8C BuNo 146991 survived the 1967–68 *Oriskany* deployment, but six other Crusaders from the unit did not. The fighter, in the spotless condition befitting its assignment to unit CO Cdr Jack Finney, is seen on the transient ramp at NAS North Island, in San Diego, shortly after VF-111 returned home on January 31, 1968. The F-8's fuselage, 18ft longer than the MiG-17F's, reduced its turning circle comparatively. Their wingspans were more comparable, the Crusader's being four feet wider than the MiG-17's 31ft 7in. (US Navy)

CHAPTER 2
SETTING THE SCENE

The Crusader's unprecedented speed and striking appearance made it a charismatic fighter from the outset. F-4 Phantom II MiG killer Jerry "Devil" Houston recalled seeing one for the first time in 1958:

> I was an ensign in my first fighter squadron, VF-173, which was equipped with the FJ-3M Fury. We were flying air-to-air gunnery sorties from [NAS] Mayport [Florida]. Several of us were lounging on the grass outside the operations building waiting for our next gunnery range times when a Crusader came into the break. I'd never seen one before, and all of us stood to watch it in the pattern and come in to land. Only the unwinding engine noise at touchdown clued us of a welcomed closer look. But at what? The sleek-in-break fighter had gone ugly. That "buzzard on a tree-limb" look was an acquired appreciation well beyond my FJ Fury taste.
>
> My attention shifted quickly to the dismounting pilot. What kind of superhero would get to fly such a plane? A handsome young man named [Lt] Dwight Timm had been diverted east to avoid a thunderstorm over [NAS] Cecil Field [also in Florida]. Super planes and heroes are easily remembered even from 64 years ago.

Houston would joined F8U-2-equipped VF-103 in March 1959. Fellow MiG killer and Crusader pilot Phil Vampatella echoed his enthusiasm for the jet:

> The F-8 was a wonderful airplane. It would really hurt you if you mistreated it, but everybody who flew it loved it.

Cdr Timm went on to lead VF-96 with F-4J Phantom IIs in 1972, becoming involved in the major aerial battles of May 10 that produced the US Navy's only Vietnam aces, Lt Randy Cunningham and Lt(jg) Willie Driscoll. "Devil" Houston, who claimed his MiG four days before Cunningham and Driscoll while flying an F-4B from VF-51 with Lt Kevin Moore as his Radar Intercept

Officer (RIO), had previously flown Crusaders in combat with VF-194 in 1966–68. In his opinion:

> The F-8 stole your heart from the get-go with its beauty and, for its time, power (God, an afterburner!), but it quickly earned an ensign-killer reputation, rightly or wrongly. In the long run, that reputation contributed greatly to fighter pilot development in the US Navy – only the top ten percent of pilots were even considered for the F-8 pipeline. And as luck would have it, a damn solid base of mid-level stick-and-throttle talent groomed the hungry youngsters into frothing-at-the-mouth tacticians.
>
> Without experiencing it, anyone would be hard pressed to understand the aura that surrounded that early F-8 community. An ensign in an F-8 took no crap from a lieutenant commander who flew anything else. Period. Among that small but growing group, anyone in the first few squadrons equipped with the F-8 knew exactly where they stood in the overall tactics ladder. Killing capability meant everything. Gunnery, tactics, gunnery, tactics, and just enough intercept training to get you into the sky with another victim. Everything funneled the best pilots and the best airplanes through a narrow training "spout," and out popped the world's best fighter pilots. They all ate, breathed, thought and dreamt about fighting airplanes. All the time.

After F-8 assignments with VF-103, VF-194, VF-124 and VF-51, Jerry "Devil" Houston (seen here as a lieutenant commander) transitioned to the F-4B with VF-51 in 1972 and scored a MiG-17 victory on May 6 that same year. (US Navy)

Prior to the aircraft drawing blood in the skies over North Vietnam, Crusader pilots had come close to fighting MiG-15s and MiG-17s, or even the occasional MiG-21, in the aftermath of the 1962 Cuban Missile Crisis in October 1962. Cuban pilots were in the habit of harassing unarmed RF-8As of VFP-62 conducting Operation *Blue Moon* photo-reconnaissance missions over international waters, resulting in F-8Es from VF-62 and F-4Bs from VMFA(AW)-531 being scrambled from NAS Key West, Florida, to chase them off. On several occasions the MiGs were perfect Sidewinder targets, but they had to be allowed to escape back into their own airspace.

US Navy and US Marine Corps Crusaders had been deployed to Southeast Asia on board aircraft carriers assigned to the Seventh Fleet from 1961 for deterrent purposes following political unrest in Laos. In May 1962, eight Crusaders from VMF-451 that had deployed to NAF Atsugi, Japan, four months earlier embarked in USS *Hancock* (CVA-19) to reinforce Carrier Air Group (CVG) 21 (which included F8U-1-equipped VF-211). By 1964, when hostilities in the region intensified, four "27C Essex-class" carriers, *Oriskany*, USS *Ticonderoga* (CVA-14), *Hancock*, and USS *Bon Homme Richard* (CVA-31) operated Crusader squadrons from their flightdecks, and they continued to do so throughout the conflict in Vietnam, rather than the heavier F-4 Phantom II for which they were not suited. USS *Shangri-La* (CVS-38) joined Task Force (TF) 77 in March 1970 with two F-8 squadrons – VF-111 and VF-162 – embarked as part of Carrier Air Wing (CVW) 8 for a single combat cruise.

A total of nine US Navy F-8 squadrons and the US Marine Corps' VMF(AW)-212 made numerous wartime deployments aboard Essex-class

Veteran "27C Essex-class" carriers like *Hancock*, seen here during its WestPac cruise in late 1963, were home to no fewer than nine F-8 units during the Vietnam War. Eight F-8As from VF-211 are visible in this photograph, as are three RF-8As from VFP-63 Det L. The A-model Crusaders, along with the F-3B Demons of VF-213 and the A-4Bs of VA-212 chained down on the flightdeck, were undertaking their final operational deployment with CVG-21 (which became CVW-21 on December 20, 1963 – four days after the cruise had ended). (US Navy)

"boats," while VF-111 was embarked in the larger USS *Kitty Hawk* (CVA-63) on a WestPac with Seventh Fleet in the first half of 1964. It had been replaced by F-4B/G-equipped VF-213 by the time the carrier departed on its first combat cruise in October 1965. CVW-15, embarked in USS *Coral Sea* (CVA-43), controlled a mixed fighter force off North Vietnam in 1964–65 when F-8D "day fighters" of VF-154 shared the flightdeck with F-4B "all-weather interceptors" of VF-151. CVW-2, embarked in *Coral Sea*'s sister-ship USS *Midway* (CVA-41), similarly had F-8Ds of VF-111 sharing fighter duties with F-4Bs of VF-21 for its 1965 combat cruise.

Finally, VF-111 twice supplied three aircraft to CVW-10 as Detachment 11 (christened "Omar's Orphans") to provide fighter escort for RF-8G missions flown by VFP-63 Det 11 from USS *Intrepid* (CVS-11) during the vessel's combat cruises in 1967–68. Det 11, led by future F-4 MiG killer Lt Cdr Foster S. Teague, also included Lt Tony Nargi, who made the final confirmed MiG kill for an F-8 on September 19, 1968 while flying from *Intrepid*.

By 1964 the Crusader had been replaced by the Phantom II in all but two Atlantic Fleet units (VF-13 and VF-62), so F-8 activities were concentrated in the Pacific Fleet until the last frontline fighter examples (F-8Js flown by VF-191 and VF-194) were finally supplanted by F-4s in 1976 when *Oriskany* was decommissioned. VF-124 at NAS Miramar, California, was the Pacific Fleet Replacement Squadron until 1972 (after which co-located VFP-63 took the tasking on), while VF-174 performed this role for the Atlantic Fleet at NAS Cecil Field until 1966.

Seventh Fleet's carrier air wings accomplished extraordinary levels of activity over Vietnam. *Oriskany*'s CVW-16 alone flew 181 large-scale strikes on the most heavily defended areas around Hanoi and Haiphong during two cruises (in 1966 and 1967–68). Its squadrons participated in the first attacks on the MiG base at Phuc Yen, the port of Cam Pha, and the shipyards at Haiphong, as well as major bridge targets in the attempt to cut off North Vietnam's supply routes to South Vietnam. The cost was considerable. In that time CVW-16 lost 60 aircraft in combat and had serious damage inflicted to a further 52. Almost a quarter of its pilots were either killed in action or taken prisoner. Of those who survived, many suffered the long-term effects of combat stress, some succumbing to heart attacks in their forties and others to the early onset of fatal diseases.

Crusader involvement in the war began with VFP-63 RF-8A detachments Det C, operating from *Kitty Hawk*, and Det E, embarked in *Bon Homme Richard*, providing photo-reconnaissance over Laos and Vietnam from May 1964 during an operation codenamed *Yankee Team*. In April of that year, ten F-8Es from VF-51 had supplanted F-4Bs of VF-142 and VF-143 assigned to CVW-14 and embarked in USS *Constellation* (CVA-64) expressly to escort RF-8As of VFP-63's Det F on photo-reconnaissance missions over Laos.

Despite F-8s from both VF-51 and VF-111 routinely using rockets and guns in an effort to suppress Laotian anti-aircraft artillery (AAA) fire during this period, the latter became so severe that Lt Charles Klusmann of VFP-63 Det C was

shot down on 6 June 1964. An F-8D flown by VF-111 CO Cdr Doyle Lynn was downed by AAA the following day during another RF-8A escort mission. Twenty RF-8s would eventually be lost in combat in Southeast Asia, although none fell to MiGs.

Zuni rockets as F-8 weapons were introduced to battle by CVW-5's VF-51 and VF-53 embarked in *Ticonderoga* when they were used to respond to an attack by three North Vietnamese Navy (NVN) motor torpedo boats on USS *Maddox* (DD-731) undertaking a DESOTO signals intelligence collecting patrol in the Gulf of Tonkin on August 2, 1964. CVW-5's F-8Es, led by the CO of the carrier air wing, Cdr James Bond Stockdale (who had a "007" call-sign and was the first pilot to clock up 1,000 hours on Crusaders), were called in to attack the torpedo boats. They strafed all three, leaving them badly damaged. A second attack on August 4, although unproven, led to retaliatory Operation *Pierce Arrow* strikes on four NVN motor torpedo boat bases and an oil storage depot at Vinh the following day. A total of 64 sorties were flown by aircraft from CVW-5 and CVW-14, with the operation being led by Stockdale's F-8s.

During the first war cruises undertaken by sister-ships *Coral Sea* and *Midway*, their embarked carrier air wings controlled a mixed fighter force of F-8D "day fighters" and F-4B "all-weather" interceptors. A variety of aircraft types from CVW-15 crowd *Coral Sea's* flightdeck on January 16, 1965 as the vessel sails off Hawaii bound for the South China Sea and 167 days on the line with TF 77. Seventeen Crusaders from VF-154 and VFP-63 Det D can be seen. CVW-15 would lose no fewer than 23 of its aircraft (including nine Crusaders) during *Coral Sea's* 11-month WestPac. (US Navy)

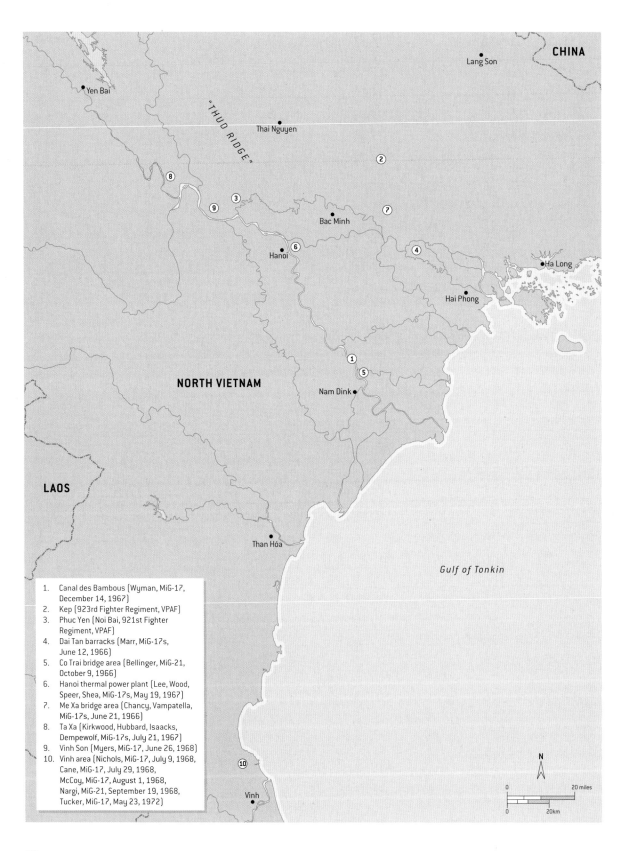

CHINA

Lang Son

Yen Bai

"THUD RIDGE"

Thai Nguyen

② 2

⑧ 8

③ 3

⑨ 9

⑦ 7

Bac Minh

④ 4

Ha Long

⑥ 6

Hanoi

Hai Phong

NORTH VIETNAM

① 1

⑤ 5

Nam Dink

LAOS

Than Hóa

Gulf of Tonkin

1. Canal des Bambous (Wyman, MiG-17, December 14, 1967)
2. Kep (923rd Fighter Regiment, VPAF)
3. Phuc Yen (Noi Bai, 921st Fighter Regiment, VPAF)
4. Dai Tan barracks (Marr, MiG-17s, June 12, 1966)
5. Co Trai bridge area (Bellinger, MiG-21, October 9, 1966)
6. Hanoi thermal power plant (Lee, Wood, Speer, Shea, MiG-17s, May 19, 1967)
7. Me Xa bridge area (Chancy, Vampatella, MiG-17s, June 21, 1966)
8. Ta Xa (Kirkwood, Hubbard, Isaacks, Dempewolf, MiG-17s, July 21, 1967)
9. Vinh Son (Myers, MiG-17, June 26, 1968)
10. Vinh area (Nichols, MiG-17, July 9, 1968, Cane, MiG-17, July 29, 1968, McCoy, MiG-17, August 1, 1968, Nargi, MiG-21, September 19, 1968, Tucker, MiG-17, May 23, 1972)

⑩ 10

Vinh

N

0   20 miles

0   20km

Typifying the ground attack role that occupied most Crusader squadrons in 1965, F-8E BuNo 147056 of VF-111 pulls out at the end of a strafing run over South Vietnam. Delivered to VF-111 in 1962, this jet survived the war and subsequent service with the Philippine Air Force and is presently on display at Manila-Aquino Airport. (Terry Panopalis Collection)

The pilot of a VF-211 F-8E signals that he is ready for launch from *Hancock* in the spring of 1965 during the carrier's last of five periods on the line with TF 77. The IR search and track sensor ahead of the jet's windscreen occasionally gave the pilot a tactical advantage when undertaking ACM training with F-4s, as it could pick up the latter jet's engine heat at a range of more than 20 miles. However, once F-8 units entered combat over Southeast Asia, it was generally seen as an adjunct to the Crusader's radar as the IR sensor suffered from poor reliability. (US Navy)

The first aerial combat between a Crusader and a MiG occurred on April 3, 1965 when four *Hancock*-embarked F-8Es from VF-211 provided flak suppression for A-4s targeting a bridge. Making their first appearance in combat, four 921st Fighter Regiment (FR) MiG-17s were vectored behind Lt Cdr Spence Thomas and his wingman. Evading the F-4 MiGCAP flight, two of the VPAF pilots hit Thomas' F-8E in several places, destroying its utility hydraulics and obliging him to make an emergency landing at Da Nang.

As the US Navy became more involved in the Vietnam conflict, F-4Bs claimed their first four MiG kills between April and June 1965. Long-range, radar-guided AIM-7D Sparrows were used for all four victories, and at least two kills, by VF-21, were achieved in textbook head-on engagements in which the MiGs did not maneuver to avoid the missiles. From then until June 1966, the majority of the MiG kills fell to USAF F-4C units, which scored seven victories. Finally, on June 12, Cdr "Hal" Marr, leading VF-211 on its second Vietnam cruise embarked in *Hancock*, destroyed the first MiG-17s to fall to the F-8 community. Two more successes were credited to VF-211 just nine days later, before the next F-4B victory on July 13, 1966. Over the following 26 months, the Crusader would shoot down twice as many MiGs as the Phantom II.

CHAPTER 3
PATH TO COMBAT

As late as August 1972, the USAF called upon US Navy F-8 squadrons for tactics exchanges, with Crusader pilots providing several weeks of air-to-air combat training for F-4 Phantom II crews at Udorn RTAFB, in Thailand, in the wake of MiG-21 engagements that had resulted in a seven-to-two kill ratio in the VPAF's favor in June and a "draw" in July. Lt Cdr John B. Nichols, a VF-191 MiG killer with 350 F-8 missions in his logbook and one of only five pilots to log more than 3,000 hours in the Crusader, took two pilots from VF-211 and one from VF-24 (both units were embarked in *Hancock* as part of CVW-21 at the time) to Udorn to establish some rules for tackling the aggressive VPAF MiG-21 pilots.

Once in Thailand, Nichols found the existing, predictable tactics employed by the F-4 crews to be "terrible," focusing on Sparrow missile launching, lack of maneuvering in the vertical plane, and closely packed, inflexible "finger-four" combat formations that made two pilots in each flight easy targets for their VPAF counterparts. The F-8 contingent, confident in their own air-to-air training unlike many USAF pilots, did their best to rectify the situation. They were dismayed by the overall response, however, and returned to their carrier when the USAF insisted that they apply a weighty coat of camouflage paint to the two F-8s they had taken ashore before they were allowed to enter combat.

Although Udorn's pilots had appreciated the Naval Aviators' advice, *Red Flag* exercises, where those tactics were fully incorporated, did not begin at Nellis AFB, in Nevada, until November 1975. By then, the Navy Fighter Weapons School (NFWS), better known as Topgun, where F-8 pilots served as instructors from the outset, had been running for six years.

The value of the F-8 pilots' experience derived from a focus on aggressive air combat maneuvering (ACM) tactics, which were basic to their training and attitudes. In Vietnam, MiG killers like Lt Cdr Bob Kirkwood regularly saw US Navy pilots successfully maneuvering their F-8s against lighter, more nimble MiG-17s. Gunnery then took up an unusually large proportion of the VF-124 training syllabus, making the unit virtually unique among US Navy fighter squadrons at the time.

Early F8U-1 pilots had learned gunnery skills with the Fleet Air Gunnery Unit (FAGU), established at NAAS El Centro, California, in May 1952. Having moved to MCAS Yuma, Arizona, in June 1959, FAGU had been disestablished in February 1960 when missiles were seen as the only suitable armament for US Navy fighters. Extra gunnery training for Category 1 combat-ready pilots was now seemingly unnecessary. FAGU's Fleet Air Gunnery Meet, first held in 1956, which provided fighter pilots with the chance to discuss and develop their skills amongst their peers, was also abolished.

Would-be Crusader pilots destined for assignment to Pacific Fleet fighter squadrons received their conversion training with VF-124, whose "Crusader College" was initially based at Moffett Field, California. Here, the unit's Maintenance Officer, Lt Cdr Bill McJunkin, "takes his hat off" in salute to nine new replacement air group pilots (standing) who had just completed their first "fam" flights in the F8U-1/2 that afternoon (July 7, 1959). Their instructors, dubbed "Crusader College Professors," are standing behind them. (US Navy)

Dogfight Tuition

Training for most F-8 units included long sessions on ACM and time attacking targets on ranges at El Centro, Yuma, and Guantanamo Bay, Cuba, where their abilities in gunnery and tactics were constantly rated and competitively developed. Pilots learned the limitations of their range and computing AN/APS-67 radar, which required the target aircraft to maintain course and speed for a minimum of three seconds so that it could compute a solution. Training included supersonic passes from high altitude against towed "banner" targets, and ACM in which pilots fought individual opponents "one-on-one" or in other combinations.

Some pilots sustained their gunnery and dogfighting skills flying training sorties against NAS North Island-based utility squadron VU-3 off the coast of southern California. However, accurate gunnery for the F-8 – appropriately christened the "last of the gunfighters" – had to be combined with thorough training in pushing the aircraft to its limits in aerial combat.

Gunnery and night carrier landings were the most demanding skills required of an F-8 pilot. In 1958 Dan Pedersen, who would become the first CO of the NFWS a decade later, had seen how an elderly but well-flown and highly maneuverable Air National Guard F-86H Sabre could defeat both the US Navy's latest Mach 2 F8U-1 Crusader and his own highly agile F4D Skyray in a series of dogfights. He understood the vital need for intensive ACM training for close-in dogfighting with aircraft like the MiG-17 – a jet with similar characteristics to the Sabre. Unfortunately, his views were dismissed by "senior management," and such "risky" flying was actually forbidden.

With an all-red radome to mark its assignment to the CO of VF-124, F-8J BuNo 149164 prepares to enter the NAS Miramar pattern prior to landing at the end of a training flight in the mid-1960s. Built as an F8U-2NE, this aircraft spent its entire operational career with VF-124. (US Navy)

Following five months flying FJ-3Ms with VF-173, Lt(jg) Jerry Houston went through initial F8U-1 Replacement Air Group (RAG) training in late 1958 when ACM simply involved Crusaders versus Crusaders:

There was no dissimilar air-to-air training – not surprising since most fleet replacement pilots [FRPs] and more than a few RAG instructors had a comfortable margin between their maneuvering envelope and the F-8's. A few operational squadrons were initially designated as the "RAG-to-be" squadrons, despite their pilots having NO previous experience in the F-8s. That meant the original F-8 RAG instructors might have been only a few flights ahead of the new FRPs they were teaching. Later, when F-8 units returning from deployment sent their best pilots to the RAGs to serve as instructors, many of the dumb-ass mistakes made by both the FRPs and the original "instructors" in the early days were eradicated.

Early into the F-8 training syllabus newly designated Naval Aviators had to be in the top ten percent of their training command classes to be chosen for Crusader training. This "cream of the crop" decision probably saved some lives and aircraft.

Accident rates during the training of jet pilots had been very high in all US services, restricting the syllabus time devoted to ACM, where both students and their machines were pushed to their limits. Navigation exercises, air-to-ground ordnance delivery, and formation flying were prioritized, with ACM limited to a few sorties or eliminated entirely. The advent of the F-4 Phantom II long-range, missile-armed fleet defense interceptor reinforced those attitudes. The high cost of this twin-engined, two-man fighter and its expensive radar and fire control systems compared to the simpler F-8 added to a reluctance to risk the loss of such an aircraft in strenuous ACM in which airframe fatigue lives were shortened and pilots might lose control, black out, or collide.

F-8 trainees were less constricted by such concerns, although losses in training were higher than those for the F-4 as a result. Not until the introduction of the NFWS, where F-8 instructors were included in F-4 training programs at

NAS Miramar, were pilots and RIOs shown how the Phantom II could be a viable platform in traditional air-to-air combat.

The NFWS built on the lessons taught by VF-124 instructors as part of the "Crusader College" course. During the latter, would-be F-8 pilots were shown how to effectively use the jet's four Colt-Browning Mk 12 20mm cannon during close-in fighting with an opponent, rather than lobbing air-to-air missiles from long-range. They also spent long hours analyzing their air-to-air encounters to improve their performances. VF-124's initial four-week "Crusader College" course included 75 classroom hours and 25 in the air concentrating on ACM, gunnery, radar, and Sidewinder tactics.

Instructors quickly discovered that the "Sidewinder and guns" attack format worked well, since a Crusader pursuing a MiG would probably be in the right envelope for either weapon. However, a Phantom II pilot trying to catch up with a target after making a head-on Sparrow launch at long range would have to slow down and reposition for a tail-on Sidewinder launch.

Lacking the F-4's all-weather capability, Crusaders were essentially clear-air day fighters. In combat their best air-to-air results were – unsurprisingly – achieved in the summer months of 1966–68; the most favorable time for weather in Southeast Asia, which was otherwise noted for monsoon conditions and poor visibility. For F-8 pilots, clear air minimized their reliance on radar to detect targets and increased their chances of success in the early stages of an attack. Three-quarters of Crusader and Phantom II MiG kills were scored in a first attack, often before the VPAF pilots had been alerted of the fighters' presence. The rate of success enjoyed by the F-8 would have been even higher if its weapons had been more reliable.

ACM training against another F-8 usually began with a head-on pass in afterburner at 20,000ft, having initially climbed together and then separated in 30-degree turns apart. Several maximum power turns, high-G climbs and dives were then employed to get within gun range of an opponent's tail.

Gunnery practice involved a six-foot-long, bullet-shaped Styrofoam target towed on a 2,000ft steel cable behind another F-8. The target had four remotely activated flares fixed to its tail for pilots to practice Sidewinder target acquisition. Groups of up to 16 students from VF-124 would spend two weeks attending a gunnery course, undertaking shooting practice sorties twice or three times daily. They learned that closing to within 500–600ft of the target gave the guns the best chance of causing real damage, and that the F-8 was able to turn and maneuver most effectively at higher altitudes. In combat, however, they would frequently have to engage MiGs at lower altitudes.

Banner targets were towed at 20,000–30,000ft, and F-8 pilots dived supersonically from a "perch" 5,000ft higher. They would attack the target in a figure-eight pattern, using their gun-laying radar to lock onto a metal radar reflector on the banner in order to compute the correct lead angle.

VF-124's distinctive insignia, inspired by its nickname, "Crusader College." The unit had originally established as fleet fighter squadron VF-53 in August 1948, and it saw combat with F4U-4Bs in Korea. It was re-designated VF-124 at Moffett Field in April 1958 as a fleet replacement squadron, training pilots to fly the Crusader through to August 1972. The squadron commenced its transition to the F-14 Tomcat two months later. (US Navy)

Crusader pilots, whether under training or serving with a fleet unit, used towed targets to improve their aerial gunnery prowess. They could be towed behind another F-8, or, as seen here, by an A-4C Skyhawk from Fleet Composite Squadron (VC) 7 based at Miramar. The unit also had a handful of Crusaders (both DF-8A/Fs and standard F-8C/Ks) on strength, which were used as aerial controlling aircraft for missile testing at NAWS China Lake, in California. These jets were photographed near San Diego in 1969. (US Navy)

A missile engagement posed real challenges for the pilot in judging the correct range to the target and its deflection "angle off" from his heading so that his missile was correctly launched within its "envelope." Even the most experienced pilots had difficulty with this, and for those new to combat it was a very different experience from shooting at drones flying a predictable course. The AIM-9D was effective in around 60 percent of properly judged launches that were made "in envelope," but the overall success rate often fell below 20 percent.

"The Hardest Airplane"

Naval Aviators received five months of F-8 tuition with VF-124 at Miramar or (until 1966) VF-174 at Cecil Field. They were then assigned to a unit that was returning from a deployment, continuing their training until it departed on its next cruise. Pilots were expected to push their aircraft hard during training. Indeed, between 1961 and 1967 18 pilots ejected from VF-124 jets, often because they had overstressed the airframe or run low on fuel, rather than due to a technical failure. Jerry Houston explained:

> Some of the losses (both original instructors and replacement pilots) were from fuel starvation – the forgotten fuel transfer switch – or loss of control. I remember

one case of overstress in the [landing] break, with the wing departing from the aircraft at Cecil Field. Relatively few losses were as a result of mechanical failure.

One of their greatest challenges was learning to operate from the relatively small World War II-vintage Essex-class carriers, which had been fitted with angled decks as part of the Ship Characteristics Board (SCB) Program 27 of the 1950s so as to allow the vessels to handle jet aircraft. The demands of the Vietnam War caused the delayed retirement of several smaller Essex-class vessels – *Shangri-La*, *Oriskany*, *Intrepid*, *Hancock*, and *Ticonderoga* – which could not handle larger aircraft like the RA-5C Vigilante and F-4 Phantom II.

Despite the design features of the F-8 (sometimes called the "gator") that enabled acceptable landing speeds, it was still, as MiG killer Paul Speer remarked, a case of "taking the hardest airplane to bring aboard and putting it on the smallest decks." Ramp strikes – hitting the ramp with the arrestor hook or even the whole fuselage – were most common within the tight confines of the Essex carriers' landing area. This occurred 14 times during CVW-21's 1966–67 cruise on board *Hancock*. Sometimes, pilots like VF-154's Lt S. A. Jackson were able to "bolter" after a ramp strike, although his hydraulics were terminally damaged after hitting *Coral Sea*'s ramp.

Keeping the approach speed correct was crucial during the three seconds pilots had to get things exactly right before arrestment. Some Crusader pilots removed the right thumb of their flying gloves for better contact with the "coolie hat" trim buttons on the control column to finesse the aircraft's attitude on

The F-8's "gator" nickname was earned because, as one test pilot commented, "It would eat you alive if you let it." VF-154, the first West Coast fighter unit to be issued with the Crusader, had 14 major accidents with the aircraft in its first two years of operations. The F8U-1 was particularly susceptible to undercarriage collapses, arrestor hook failures, and ramp strikes because the speed margins of plus or minus two to three knots on approach were hard to maintain. Here, VF-154 F8U-1E BuNo 145466 "bolters" over *Coral Sea*'s flightdeck following a waved off approach on March 4, 1961. (US Navy)

F-8E BuNo 150352 of VF-211 launches from *Bon Homme Richard* on May 24, 1967. On a signal from the catapult officer, the deck-edge catapult operator pressed a button that allowed steam into the catapult shuttle piston chamber at around 300-psi, accelerating a 32,000lb Crusader to 130mph almost instantaneously. Lt(jg) Thomas R. Hall, with more than 100 missions logged, was shot down by AAA in this aircraft during a strike on the Bac Giang thermal power plant on June 10, 1967. He spent the rest of the war as a PoW. (US Navy)

final approach. Jerry Houston recalled that the glove modification was "not uncommon, especially in the F8U-1 and most especially after the pilot experienced his first pilot-induced oscillation from a careless trim wheel flick. Reducing the sensitivity of that trim wheel 'devil' was the most appreciated modification ever made to the Crusader."

The approach power compensator, introduced with the F-8D as the first such unit ever installed in a US Navy fighter, adjusted the throttle in response to the pilot's control movements to maintain the ideal angle of attack and acceleration on approach to the flightdeck. This device remedied the aircraft's speed instability and greatly improved safety, saving many lives. The concept was subsequently developed into the automatic carrier landing system that became standard for most US Navy aircraft.

Of the 170 F-8s lost during the conflict in Southeast Asia, 83 were destroyed in combat – primarily by AAA. A further 109 were sufficiently damaged to need major rework. Twelve of the aircraft shot down were US Marine Corps Crusaders. F-8s had an accident rate of 46.70 per 100,000 flight hours, which was more than double that of the F-4B/J (20.17 per 100,000 hours) and amongst the highest for a US tactical aircraft. In 1969, F-8s had three times as many accidents at sea as F-4s, despite there being far more of the latter aircraft in fleet service.

Unsurprisingly, 1957–58 saw the most accidents for the new type, with no fewer than nine major accidents in 3,690 hours in 1957 alone – a rate of 243.9 per 100,000 hours. VF-154, which was the first Pacific Fleet unit issued with Crusaders, suffered five fatalities in its first year (1957–58) and 14 major accidents in its first two years. 1962 was the worst year for major Crusader mishaps, with 106 occurring, but at a much lower rate of 55.8 per 100,000 hours. In 1965, the accident rate was still eight times that of the F-4B. The toll declined in most succeeding years, although rates of around 50 to 60 per 100,000 hours occurred in several years up to 1979, but overall it averaged out at 46.74 major accidents per 100,000 hours – twice that of the next highest carrier-based jet, the A-4 Skyhawk. There were 186 operational pilot losses in F-8 units.

The attrition rate was so severe in 1967 that VF-111 had to revert to flying older F-8Cs taken from utility squadrons as there were insufficient E-models available. Assigned to CVW-16 and embarked in *Oriskany*, the unit lost its bombing capability for the carrier's bloody 1967–68 combat cruise after switching to older Crusaders. No fewer than 12 F-8s were lost during this deployment, with three pilots killed and three captured.

Many operational mishaps were attributed to the pilot's inability to recover a jet from a stall or spin. In combat, the aircraft was stressed for a 6.5g limit,

although pilots regularly exceeded that in their fights with MiGs. Pilot error was also inevitably a factor. There were seven extreme cases of F-8s taking off from land bases with their outer wings still folded, although all the pilots were able to land safely, albeit with an approach speed of around 175 knots. Lt Cdr Tom Hudner was able to use negative G in flight to make his folded wings spread and lock. On one occasion, Lt Cdr Stuart Harrison of VF-62 landed successfully after his engine quit following fuel starvation 1,700ft from the flightdeck – the first ever carrier landing by a jet aircraft with a non-running engine.

"Gator" Aviators

By the time they engaged with MiGs, most F-8 squadron and division leaders had at least 3,000 hours of flight time, much of it in F-8s, while junior pilots often had more than 800 hours. Most MiG kills were achieved by the older pilots who frequently had the best firing opportunities as leaders. Twelve fell to commanders or lieutenant commanders and six to lieutenants.

As CO of VF-211, which amassed eight MiG kills to make it the joint highest scoring US Navy squadron (with F-4-equipped VF-96) of the war, Cdr Paul Speer – who had flown F2H Banshees in the Korean War – was widely respected. His squadron included some unusually skillful pilots whose achievements typified the importance of strong morale and relationships within the unit as a factor in promoting aggressive, coordinated tactics in combat involving both experienced flyers and "new guys."

Many Naval Aviators would build their experience by completing two or more consecutive combat deployments, while most MiG pilots remained in frontline units for the duration of the war. Their Soviet training was usually briefer and more focused on following rigid instructions from

In a famously well-photographed arrestment mishap lasting a few seconds, Lt(jg) John Kryway ejects from his almost new VF-11 F8U-1 in October 21, 1961. A hard landing on the rising deck of USS *Franklin D. Roosevelt* (CVA-42) caused his starboard magnesium main landing gear to fracture and ignite. A broken arrestor hook left instant ejection as the only alternative. Quick-thinking Kryway was recovered safely. (US Navy)

Ground Control Interception (GCI) personnel during their short-ranged interception sorties.

Pushing the F-8's maneuverability to its limits was an essential skill to master. In some ways the A-4 – a vital type in Topgun programs – was better for weaving and turning with MiGs. Several Skyhawk pilots found themselves in good positions for gun attacks on MiG-17s over North Vietnam, but they lacked an afterburner for vertical fights and their defensive armament was limited to one or two 20mm guns and very little ammunition. Nevertheless, two MiG-17s were downed by A-4 pilots.

For Naval Aviators flying the F-8, the ability to climb at a 70-degree angle was often the best way to dominate a fight. In Vietnam most Crusader versus MiG engagements took place at relatively low altitudes. Pilot training prioritized safety in order to allow for recovery from situations where loss of control might occur. Higher altitudes were therefore advocated. Jerry Houston recalled:

> I can't remember an ACM briefs that didn't mention a 10,000ft "safety" deck, and that was purely due to the F-8's history departing controlled flight and requiring more than a little altitude to recover. There were no demonstrations, or practices, of spins or recoveries in the F-8. Nevertheless, in combat there was never any hesitancy to drop to treetop level, as need be, for MiGs.

Avoiding afterburner use to reduce visibility or recognizing reflections from the windscreen or shiny surfaces of an opposing fighter could give a pilot an initial advantage in an engagement. Similarly, small problems could make a fight much more difficult. During Dick Schaffert's epic dogfight described in the first chapter, a high-G break forced his oxygen mask and microphone down over his chin. Subsequently preoccupied with ten minutes of strenuous maneuvers, he could not adjust it and radio for assistance from other Crusaders.

Pilots who had the comparatively rare opportunity to shoot down a MiG would receive a Silver Star, the US military's third highest award for valor in combat, and also considerable kudos that often led to promotions. Initially, such successes received widespread Press coverage, encouraged by the US Navy, but as the war progressed media interest declined and some pilots avoided publicity in case their families were harassed by anti-war protesters.

Considering their unbeaten wartime record of kills-per-engagement, their accurate use of Sidewinders within the missile's launch envelope and their willingness to engage MiGs in turning fights, F-8 pilots were considered to be the best air-to-air pilots in-theater during Operation *Rolling Thunder* by leading air combat analyst and USAF Phantom II Vietnam War pilot Marshall Michel. Their outstanding score of 14 kills in 1967–68 for no losses to MiGs speaks for itself.

Cdr Paul Speer led VF-211 to great aerial success during *Bon Homme Richard*'s second war cruise, with the unit claiming four of the nine MiG-17s credited to CVW-21 in 1967. He downed one of four "Red bandits" destroyed by F-8s during the May 19 Walleye attack on the Bac Giang thermal power plant. (US Navy)

CHAPTER 4
WEAPON OF WAR

Vought's F8U Crusader was designed at a time when existing US Navy fighters were substantially outclassed by the Soviet MiG-15. Early supersonic American designs like the F3H Demon were severely limited by their inadequate Westinghouse J40 engines. Vought's own tail-less F7U Cutlass was also dogged by engine problems and delays that threatened the company's future as a US Navy supplier. The F8U was developed at the same time as the USAF's F-100 Super Sabre, and both aircraft were designed around the superior Pratt & Whitney J57 engine in airframes that were configured for true supersonic interception. However, the F8U-1, which was around 4,500lb lighter than the F-100, became a true dogfighter while the Super Sabre was quickly assigned to ground attack roles during the conflict in Southeast Asia.

Chance M. Vought himself had designed the US Navy's first purpose-built aircraft, the VE-9, in 1921. Working with Frederick Rentschler, founder of the Pratt & Whitney company, Vought's Chief Engineer, Rex Beisel, led a team that conceived the F4U Corsair in the late 1930s. It eventually matured into one of the most successful fighters of World War II, and also saw widespread use as a fighter-bomber in the Korean War.

In 1952 Vought responded to the US Navy's urgent request in its Outline Specification (OS) 130 for a single-seat, supersonic "Day Superiority Fighter" with a large fuel capacity and a slow carrier landing speed. Eight companies submitted adventurous designs for this formidable technical challenge, some with variable-sweep wings or tail-less delta formats. North American's "Super Fury," a carrier-modified Super Sabre derivative, was included.

Vought's designers, who included an unusually high proportion of former fighter pilots and engineers, examined 12 possible configurations and opted for a relatively conventional layout. The profile of its long fuselage happened to comply with the "area rule" concept relating to the proportion of fuselage length to wing area and position which produced the optimum combination for reducing transonic drag. Rival designs required alteration to incorporate a "Coke bottle" fuselage profile (resisted by Vought) to achieve the same effect.

This was considered for Vought's F8U in 1954 for additional performance but ruled out to save cost and delays.

A low-mounted, all-moving horizontal stabilizer, or "unit hydraulic tail" (UHT) enhanced controllability at high angles of attack without interference from airflow over the wing and avoided pitch-up. The cockpit was placed far forward for good visibility on landing. Space was allowed ahead of it for an APG-30 gunsight radar or a larger radar. The F8U had one of the first built-in ram-air turbines for emergency electrical power.

One of the design's most innovative features was the high-mounted wing that could be raised by +7 degrees at its leading edge to provide the correct angle of attack for carrier take-off and landing. It required an unusually strong hinge, but the high wing permitted a very short undercarriage, while still allowing for under-wing stores and giving easy access for maintenance. Under heavy G-loads the fuselage and wings would flex visibly and under extreme loads the entire wing could separate from the aircraft.

The variable-incidence wing allowed the fuselage to be at an angle of attack of only six to eight degrees relative to the deck on final approach, giving excellent forward visibility and reducing the punishing load exerted on the nose landing gear on touch-down. It also placed the fuselage parallel with the deck for catapult take-off and allowed a low cockpit canopy profile, adding around 100mph at 35,000ft. However, the lower canopy severely reduced rearward visibility, and pilots in combat had to resort to regular ten-degree turns left and right to check their "six o'clock."

The NACA-inspired wing, swept at 42 degrees, was a complex and extremely effective structure. Its leading edge drooped 25 degrees with the wing raised. The trailing edge incorporated large "flaperons" (combined flaps and ailerons) to prevent the "control reversal" problems experienced by a number of swept-wing jets when their outboard ailerons made the wing flex, causing the ailerons to have the opposite effect to that required. They drooped by 20 degrees for take-off and landing, linked automatically to the wing incidence position and leading edge "droops." Smaller inboard flaps reduced landing speed further, and a dogtooth in the leading edge where the outer, folding wing section was attached – the first production use of this device – acted like a stabilizing wing fence at high speeds.

An additional landing speed reduction of six knots through boundary layer control – blowing engine bleed air over the ailerons and flaps – was proposed in 1955, tested in mid-1957, and, eventually, incorporated in the F-8J (modernized F-8E Crusader) and the French Navy's F-8E(FN) version.

The main wing structure was a box with machined integral stiffening that contained half the 1,188 US gallons of internal JP-5 fuel. The eight-tank capacity fulfilled long-range interception requirements but also (in an addition to the original OS-130 parameters) fed a fuel-guzzling afterburner to enable speeds of up to Mach 1.3.

Four Colt-Browning Mk 12 20mm guns were installed in the nose with 84 rounds per gun (later increased to 150). As an additional interception weapon, an extending box beneath the forward fuselage held 32 2.75 in. Mighty Mouse unguided rockets. Engineers calculated that a fighter would have difficulty in sustaining 5g throughout its firing run, keeping its fire control system locked

onto a target at 40,000ft and 450 knots. The box extended for one second to release the rockets, at which point the aircraft's fire control system raised the nose slightly, giving the missiles a straight flightpath to blast heavy bomber targets with a "shotgun" effect.

In 1952, the US Navy saw the guns-and-rockets combination as appropriate "to destroy opposing fighters in the air or on the ground." Six years later, tests with the rockets revealed that they tended to collide when salvoed, shedding debris that could enter the Crusader's engine inlet. The launch sequence was extended to increase separation. In 1955, an alternative package containing four shortened AIM-9 Sidewinders in an internal bay was considered. In November 1952 four underwing Sperry Sparrow guided air-to-air missiles were proposed, although this option was not pursued. Later plans proposed two wingtip or pylon-mounted Sparrows, but the smaller AIM-9 was clearly a more practical choice for a day fighter. Sidewinders on fuselage pylons were tested on F8U-1 BuNo 141343 in 1956.

In 1955, the US Navy specified in-flight refueling for its carrier-based aircraft. Lack of internal space necessitated a bulged fairing on the F8U-1's left fuselage side for a retracting refueling probe, tested on BuNo 141346 in 1957 and incorporated in production aircraft from airframe 66. The F8U-1P reconnaissance Crusader's probe was internal without the bulge.

Despite its initial requirement for a fighter design demonstrating "simplicity, small size, low cost and a maximum speed of Mach 1," the US Navy accepted Vought's proposal, then known as the V-383 in its J57-powered form, as the only one likely to defeat the MiG-15 and its successors. By November 1952 OS-130 allowed for greater weight and size, although the overall dimensions had to enable 25 fighters to be "spotted" (parked) within 200ft of carrier flightdeck space. The US Navy certainly saw Vought's as the only extant proposal capable of sustained supersonic speed and able to match, or preferably out-perform, the USAF's land-based interceptors, unlike previous carrier-capable fighters.

A parallel Vought design, the V-384, used the less powerful Wright J65 engine with 11,000lbs of afterburning thrust, but the Pratt & Whitney J57-P-4 was clearly superior, offering an additional 5,000 lbs of afterburning thrust and wide acceptance for several other key USAF and US Navy designs.

The Crusader's wing incidence could be changed by a single hydraulic actuator (clearly visible here), attached to the wing by one bolt. F-8C BuNo 145582 of VF-91 is on final approach to USS *Ranger* (CVA-61) during the carrier's 1962–63 WestPac with CVG-9. C-model Crusaders equipped three Pacific Fleet squadrons during the Vietnam War, and they were mainly assigned escort and CAP roles because they lacked underwing pylons. (US Navy)

The J57 was the first US engine to exceed 10,000lbs of thrust, using a twin-spool, 16-stage compressor in an axial flow design. Vought designed an air intake that avoided stalls, gave a small frontal area and allowed for radar and other equipment to be installed above it.

On June 30, 1953, three V-383 (XF8U-1) prototypes were ordered. Conscious of their reputation-damaging Cutlass program, Vought prioritized punctuality for the new aircraft. Wind tunnel tests revealed problems with directional stability, speed brake positioning, and excess drag. Consequent refinements included a reduction in the tailplane area by no less than seven square feet. Mock-up approval occurred in September 1953, although the poor rearward visibility for the pilot was noted. The three 20mm guns under the nose were replaced by pairs on each side. Construction of the first XF8U-1 (BuNo 138899) began in February 1954 at the Vought plant in Dallas, Texas. After ground testing it was taken to Muroc (Edwards) AFB, in California, on March 2, 1955 for flight testing, with the company's future in jeopardy if it failed.

Vought Chief Test Pilot John W. Konrad poses with XF8U-1 BuNo 138899 in 1955. A former USAAF B-17 Flying Fortress bomber pilot who saw action with the Eighth Air Force in World War II, he flew most of Vought's jet aircraft on their first flights. (Peter Mersky Collection)

Fortunately, the first flight, on March 25, after only 22 months of intensive work since contract signing, was a great success, and it fulfilled the team's wish to be first to go supersonic on a maiden flight. Vought Chief Test Pilot John W. Konrad took the XF8U-1 to Mach 1.1, "which was easily accomplished," finding that acceleration through the transonic region "was smooth, pleasant and rapid." Upon returning after 52 minutes, he commented, "Thanks a lot for a good airplane." The US Navy had its first 1,000mph fighter, and it handled well too. The award of the Robert J. Collier Trophy to Vought in 1956 recognized this achievement.

Testing revealed a few relatively minor problem areas that needed addressing, including the redesign of the speed brake (relocated to a position below the forward fuselage to improve stability) and the addition of nosewheel steering. The second XF8U-1 (BuNo 138900) joined the program in June 1955, and the aircraft was officially named Crusader two months later. Further minor faults including poor afterburner light-up at high altitude were highlighted and remedied during the US Navy's Phase I and II evaluations.

The first production F8U-1 (BuNo 140444) became the demonstrator Crusader, and it was also the first to be lost, killing test pilot Harry Brackett. A

failed aileron hinge appears to have initiated a series of out-of-control oscillations, culminating in the entire wing tearing off. A second loss involving the seventh F8U-1 was caused by severe pitch down, leading to structural failure and disintegration. The pilot, Maj J. A. Felton of the US Marine Corps, escaped, but the test program was delayed. John Konrad also survived ejecting when the 14th production F8U-1's engine failed to relight during maximum thrust tests.

As with most other US Navy fighters, the F8U was also offered as a photo-reconnaissance aircraft early in its development. The US Navy duly requested a mock-up of the F8U-1P (later re-designated RF-8A) by April 1955, with the first flight of the prototype, BuNo 141363, on December 17, 1956. The forward fuselage was modified to accommodate cameras at five stations and a smaller UHT was fitted. The aircraft carried 1,500lbs more fuel than the fighter version and it was faster. Photo Crusaders became vital assets in US Navy and US Marine Corps service, with the last examples retiring from a Reserve unit in March 1987. However, the US Navy rejected the proposed F8U-1T two-seat trainer ("Twosader") version. The sole example, BuNo 143710, re-designated NTF-8A, was used by the US Navy and NASA for test work, after which it helped train Philippine Air Force Crusader pilots in the late 1970s.

Four carrier-borne evaluation cruises in 1956 showed that the Crusader was hard to keep "on speed" for carrier landings. Without the angled deck and mirror landing system added to upgraded World War II-vintage SCB-27C Essex- and Midway-class carriers, the aircraft might never have reached the required safety standards. However, it was accepted for service, and its other characteristics were praised.

Between August 1956 and July 1957 several international speed records were established, including Project *Beta* – an attempt to win the Thompson

VF-154 was the first operational Crusader unit to complete carrier qualification (in November–December 1957), albeit with several deck incidents. This barrier engagement by Lt(jg) John Miottel (his second in the Crusader) occurred on June 20, 1958, during VF-154's first WestPac with the F8U as part of CVG-15 embarked in *Hancock*. The nylon barrier inevitably damaged the airframe, and in this view deep cuts can be seen into the vertical stabilizer and wing fold areas of F8U-1 BuNo 143796. (US Navy)

Trophy for the world speed record. Cdr R. W. "Duke" Windsor set a new US level flight speed record of 1,015mph, which was the first such record for a US Navy jet and the first time an American-built fighter had exceeded 1,000mph. In July 1957 Maj John Glenn flew the photo-reconnaissance F8U-1P BuNo 144608 in Project *Bullet*, a transcontinental supersonic record flight, remaining in afterburner for much of the 3hrs 23min flight.

The first production F8U-1 (BuNo 140444), re-designated F-8A from September 18, 1962, was delivered on September 20, 1955, and the type entered service with VF-32 at NAS Cecil Field the following year. The unit eventually undertook the Crusader's first carrier deployment (to the Mediterranean) from February 1, 1958 when it embarked in USS *Saratoga* (CVA-60) with CVG-3. By then, F8U-1s had also been issued to VF-154 at NAS Miramar and VMF(AW)-122 at MCAS Beaufort, in South Carolina, with the latter becoming the first US Marine Corps unit to carrier qualify in the Crusader in 1958, closely followed by VMF(AW)-235 and VMF-251.

Later Crusaders

The F8U-2 (F-8C from September 1962), proposed in mid-1957, included the AN/APS-67 search and track radar also fitted in the preceding F8U-1E (F-8B), AN/AWG-3 armament control system, and a lighter, more accurate EX-16 fire control system. Two ventral fins were added for improved supersonic directional stability, although MiG-killer "Tim" Hubbard felt that they slightly impeded maneuverability at lower speeds. Pilots were told that early versions without the fins would become dangerously unstable above Mach 1.7.

The J57-P-16 engine was specified, two external air scoops were attached to the upper rear fuselage for better afterburner cooling, and the inflight refueling probe was installed. Single-round Sidewinder rails or launchers for Zuni missiles were added to either side of the forward fuselage. From 1965, "Y" pylons for two Sidewinders could replace the single-round rails. The four-missile armament became common, particularly for squadrons flying combat missions in Southeast Asia.

As previously noted, F-8Ds equipped VF-154 embarked in *Coral Sea* and VF-111 on board *Midway* for their first combat cruises in 1964–65. The D-model (initially designated F8U-2N) was fitted with a J57-P-20 engine, uprated to 18,000lbs of afterburning thrust, and an AN/APQ-83 radar, together with a three-axis autopilot. The retractable rocket pack was replaced by a 75 US gallon fuel tank. This variant was optimized for all-weather interception, and the F8U-2NE (F-8E) took that process further with the more powerful AN/APQ-94 radar, housed in an enlarged radome. The new radar, initially tested in F8U-2NE BuNo 147036, increased the aircraft's tracking range to 30 miles and was less susceptible to ground clutter interference at low altitudes.

The pilot had a complex double pistol grip control column incorporating 31 functions. The rear section controlled the radar, while the section nearest to him was for flight control, trim, stores release, and gun firing. A small AAS-15 infrared (IR) search and track seeker was mounted above the radome to "see" hot jet pipes and jet engines in the 3- to 5-micron range at distances approaching 15 miles, enabling the fighter to track targets without using radar.

Their improved radar gave F-8Es nightfighting capability, whereas the F-8Cs, often partnered with them, were restricted to day fighter operations only.

The E-model Crusader, which flew with eight US Navy squadrons on 22 wartime deployments, and subsequent variants had two underwing pylons for 4,000lbs of ordnance. The US Marines Corps regularly used this capability for heavy bombs, but it was less common for US Navy Crusaders to carry such ordnance except in "maximum effort" missions like the one on November 17, 1965, when VF-194 F-8Es flying from *Bon Homme Richard* dropped Mk 84 2,000lb bombs on the Hai Duong bridge near Hanoi. The squadron CO, Cdr Robert Chew, was shot down after delivering his bombs, as was F-8E pilot Capt Ross Chaimson from VMF(AW)-212, embarked in *Oriskany*, who was also hit by AAA during the same operation. He was quickly rescued.

Following the November 1968 "bombing halt" with the end of Operation *Rolling Thunder*, which severely restricted strikes on targets in North Vietnam, US Navy Crusaders were subsequently scheduled for ground attack and escort sorties that seldom took them near MiGs.

The F-8E's extra weight meant that it had to reduce its fuel to the minimal "bingo" level and have little 20mm ammunition left aboard if it had to land back on the carrier with four Sidewinders still loaded. Pilots flying reworked F-8Js sometimes had to expend unused ammunition in order to meet the required landing weight. F-8Es made 12 of the Crusader's MiG kills.

US Navy F-8Es and reworked F-8Js were routinely called upon to drop dumb bombs from carriers assigned to TF 77. This meant that replacement pilots had to be trained in the art of dive-bombing, as seen here. These J-model jets were assigned to VFP-63 when the unit took over the Pacific Fleet Replacement Squadron tasking in 1972 after VF-124 commenced transitioning to the F-14. They were photographed that year dropping four Mk 82 500lb bombs on the Chocolate Mountain Aerial Gunnery Range in California. (US Navy)

Reworked Crusaders

Although it was replaced by the F-4 on larger carriers, the F-8 was still needed to boost fighter numbers on Essex-class vessels. However, by 1968, many war-weary airframes were approaching the end of their fatigue lives. Vought was requested to remanufacture 426 surviving jets beginning with 53 RF-8As. With new wings incorporating stores pylon hardpoints, J57-P-20 engines, an electronic countermeasures (ECM) package, and ventral strakes, they became much-needed RF-8Gs from August 1965. Twenty more were remanufactured in 1968–70.

Eighty-nine F-8Ds were also "re-lifed" as F-8Hs and 136 F-8Es became F-8Js with BLC using engine compressor bleed air to artificially increase wing lift. Their 2,000lbs of extra weight and ECM gear reduced ammunition storage space. BLC also reduced engine thrust by 1,000lbs so that afterburner was needed to recover from a failed landing approach. For pilots like Lt Cole Pierce, this made the F-8J "flat-out dangerous" on approach in high Southeast Asian temperatures. They could launch AGM-12 Bullpup short-range air-to-ground missiles, although this weapon was not used operationally.

The final batch of upgraded Crusaders comprised 61 F-8Bs and 87 F-8Cs which became F-8Ls and F-8Ks, respectively, from December 1968. They had the new 4,000 hours wing, but retained their original engines. For WestPac combat deployments, seven squadrons flew F-8Js and four had F-8Hs.

Weapons

The Colt-Browning Mk 12 20mm gun installation, with each weapon firing 600 rounds per minute, was the Crusader's principal armament. However, in Vietnam, guns were only involved in three of the 19 MiG kills attributed to the F-8, and then in combination with missiles. AIM-9 Sidewinders were the sole weapon in the others.

Gun jamming under the stress of G-forces above 3.5g or lack of ammunition storage capacity reduced the cannons' usefulness. Ammunition was fed downwards through a feed neck where rounds could become jammed. Spent shell cases were retained in the armament bay, and they would sometimes block the ammunition feed chutes. The ammunition boxes could hold 150 rounds each for escort or ground attack sorties, although this was often reduced to 110 rounds or less. Pilots found that armor-piercing ammunition worked best against the MiG-17, as standard high explosive shells merely peeled the skin off the airframe.

The gunsight had difficulty in computing sufficient "lead" if the fighter pulled more than 3g. Cannon lent the Crusader its "Last of the Gunfighters" sobriquet in a fighter world which was turning to missiles, but they suffered from a number of persistent problems during its combat career. Jamming was common if the fighter exceeded 1g when maneuvering, although this could be partially alleviated by reducing the number of rounds for each gun to lighten the load on the feed mechanisms. The guns also suffered from a vulnerable pneumatic charging system and "barrel whip," which caused the bullets to disperse too widely. Finally, the cannons' rate of fire sometimes slowed down or stopped altogether, despite strenuous efforts by the maintainers to improve reliability.

A VF-24 report noted that "the F-8C 20mm weapon system proved unsatisfactory under prolonged combat conditions. Although one MiG-17 was downed by cannon fire, it was done

A red-shirted ordnanceman loads the starboard Colt-Browning Mk 12 20mm cannon of an F-8E from VF-162 during *Oriskany*'s 1965 combat cruise. VF-124 instructors taught students how to make the best use of the aircraft's quartet of cannon, emphasizing that the weapons were far more effective when fired at close range. Unfortunately, the Mk 12 was plagued by reliability issues during the Vietnam conflict. (US Navy)

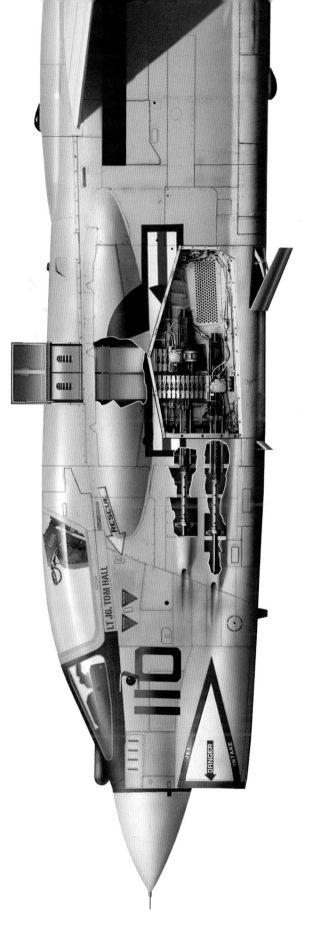

F-8 CRUSADER CANNON ARMAMENT

Although they fired 160 rounds in a two-second burst compared with 69 rounds by the MiG-17's larger-caliber cannon, the F-8's four Colt Mk 12 20mm guns delivered around a half of the weight of fire of the MiG's three weapons – 35.2lbs compared with 70.3lbs. The MiG's armament was longer-ranging and could be effective at distances of up to 5,000ft but its ammunition lasted for only around five seconds, half as long as the F-8's. Reducing the number of rounds carried from 144 to less than 100 shortened the F-8's firing time to around six seconds.

When the pilot selected Master Arm Switch "On" and squeezed the trigger switch halfway on the control column in the cockpit, it opened the gun vent doors on the underside of the forward fuselage.

The smaller forward door allowed air to be "rammed" into the gun bay when the weapons were fired, forcing collected gas out through the larger, rearward-facing doors.

The F-8's four aluminum ammunition boxes were designed specifically for the aircraft, and they each carried 110 to 125 high-explosive armor-piercing 20mm cannon shells, with every fifth round a tracer. The cannons routinely jammed, especially during turns in excess of 3.5g, much to the frustration of the pilots hell bent on killing a MiG. The F-8's low ammunition capacity was solved in part by allowing pilots to select to fire only the upper or lower pairs of guns. While this decreased the number of shells being expended, it increased the weapons' firing time.

The preserved cockpit of a VMF(AW)-232 F-8E, victim of a devastating Viet Cong attack on Da Nang on July 15, 1967. The square AN/APS-67 radar scope sits immediately beneath the gunsight. Below the radar scope is the circular attitude display, surrounded by the Mach meter, altimeter, radio magnetic indicator, and rocket pack fire light. (Thierry Deutsch)

at very close range without the aid of the lead computing sight and under low-G flight conditions." Furthermore, the guns jammed during "three of eight engagements" up to September 18, 1966, although this performance was improved somewhat by "excellent preventative maintenance."

Weapon aiming was supported by data on range and target location from the F-8B's AN/APS-67 radar (replacing the AN/APG-30 gun-ranging radar of the F-8A) which scanned a section of airspace up to 16 miles ahead of the aircraft, presenting its scan on a cockpit screen. A gyro reticle image in the gunsight glass showed an aim point for guns or rockets, computed by the EX-16 fire control system using data on airspeed, angle of attack, lead angle, and acceleration among other inputs from transducers on the aircraft's nose. The F-8E's longer-ranging and more reliable AN/APQ-94 radar (or the later and less popular pulse-Doppler AN/APQ-124 in the F-8J) scanned a section of airspace up to 24 miles ahead of the aircraft and up to 45 degrees off the centerline. All the radars had poor look-down capability.

Increased SAM and AAA radar threats over North Vietnam meant that an ECM package had to occupy some of the ammunition storage space in the nose. CVW-5's Crusader units (VF-51 and VF-53) routinely loaded only 60 rounds per gun for some CAP missions over MiG territory. Even when the magazines were fully loaded, the cannon gave only 13 seconds of firing time in total. In an attempt to extend this, some squadrons rewired the firing circuits so that guns could be fired as upper or lower pairs. If jams occurred when the ammunition links separated in their chute for one gun, it was sometimes possible to re-charge the other three.

The first US Navy Crusader fighter loss from *Dixie Station* (the area off the Mekong Delta from where carriers launched strikes in support of American and South Vietnamese troops), F-8E BuNo

150657 of VF-194 on June 30, 1965 may have been brought down by one of its own guns exploding and sending debris into the engine. Although only two Vietnam MiG kills featured guns as the principal weapons involved, they were often used to distract enemy fighters into breaking off attacks.

AAM-N-7 (re-designated AIM-9B) Sidewinder IR-seeking missiles were added as secondary armament during the F8U-2's weapons tests from August 19 to October 14, 1958. The AIM-9B was loaded on F-8s flying early missions over North Vietnam, and it was involved in the October 9, 1966 MiG-21 kill by Cdr Dick Bellinger. However, it was quickly replaced by the tighter-turning Mach 2.5-capable AIM-9D IR variant mounted on an LAU-7 launcher that became available for Vietnam use during 1965.

Faster and longer-ranging, the US Navy-sponsored AIM-9D, 9.4ft long and weighing 195lbs, was used for most of the F-8's combat successes. It had an IR sensor that was cooled by nitrogen for 60 seconds immediately prior to launch so as to improve its sensitivity to heat sources and avoid distracting heat emissions from clouds or terrain. The missile's larger 24lb Mk 48 warhead projected metal fragments over a 17ft radius to cut into airframe structures. Crucially, its shorter minimum launch range and improved target sensor doubled the dimensions of its launch envelope compared with the AIM-9B.

When paired with the F-8, the AIM-9D produced the highest kill-per-engagement ratio of any US fighter in the war and the highest success rate of any American air-to-air missile in the 1965–68 period. Having trained with the AIM-9B pre-war and learned to cope with its narrow target acquisition "view," F-8 pilots were therefore less likely to fire any Sidewinders "out of envelope." The AIM-9D had a minimum launch range of 1,000ft, plus another 1,000ft for each ten degrees of "angle off" the target's tail. At sea level, its maximum effective range was one to two nautical miles, increasing by one nautical mile for every 10,000ft of altitude.

Missile selection was made with a wafer switch placed low on the central instrument panel. When pilots carried a mix of AIM-9Cs and AIM-9Ds or Zuni rockets, the pilot had to reach down and select the right rail, or "station," for each weapon from the four available on two fuselage pylons. Zuni rockets

Although the AIM-9D achieved better results than the F-8's guns, VF-24 reported that "six out of the eleven fired through 1966 that missed did so because the pilot fired them before the aircraft was in a position from which the missile could track and guide on its target." AIM-9Ds (upper) were loaded for daylight operations and the semi-active AIM-9C (lower) was added for night sorties. The latter weapon gave limited head-on launch capability, but AIM-9Cs were not used in combat and their costly maintenance problems prompted their withdrawal in 1969. (US Navy)

F-8 CRUSADER AIM-9 SIDEWINDER ARMAMENT

The AIM-9D Sidewinder (carried here on a "Y-rack") was powered by a 3,500lb thrust solid fuel rocket with a five-second burn time, reaching Mach 2.5. Fired from behind a target aircraft, the weapon was effective from a minimum range of 1,000ft to up to two miles. However, its maximum deflection angle was little more than 20 degrees, although the AIM-9D had a nominal turn capability of 18g at sea level.

The pilot received a "growl" tone in his headset to show that the Sidewinder's sensitive IR homing device was tracking a heat source, followed by a higher-pitched sound when it locked onto a heat target and was ready to launch. Sidewinders worked best when fired with clear sky as the background to the target. F-8s often flew with only two AIM-9Ds to reduce drag and ensure the minimum landing weight if the jet returned with them still aboard.

The F-8C was the first Crusader variant to have the increased firepower offered by the creation of the four-station "Y-rack" that could carry either Sidewinders or Zunis, and occasionally a mix. The "Bravo" Sidewinder weighed 167lb and the "Delta" 198lb. The warheads were, respectively, ten or 20 pounds of high-explosive. The "Delta's" range was increased to two miles over the "Bravo's" 1.2 miles. The F-8 was capable of carrying three types of Sidewinder during the Vietnam War – the AIM-9B (IR seeker head), the AIM-9D (semi-active radar IR head), and the rarely carried, trouble prone AIM-9C (semi-active radar-guided head), designed specifically for the Crusader. A surplus of "Bravos" early in the war required many squadrons assigned to TF 77 to call for the more effective, but relatively scarce "Deltas" to be ferried from one carrier to another when MiGs were expected in upcoming missions.

were aimed using the gunsight and good judgment.

Weapons shortages occurred as the number of strikes increased in 1966, and with AIM-9Ds being scarce at that point, CVW-16's F-8Es (flown by VF-111 and VF-162) regularly launched with two Sidewinders rather than four – occasionally, they carried only one. Missiles had to be swapped between carriers to share them out. AIM-9D shortages occurred once again in 1968, resulting in AIM-9Bs being substituted in their place. Ironically, VF-111 pilots, who had had to revert to the F-8C due to a shortage of E-models, found the AIM-9B's fusing system more reliable. Finally, when supplies of Mk 83 1,000lb bombs for flak suppression also ran low, they were replaced by less effective 2.75in. rockets.

Zuni five-inch diameter folding-fin projectiles were often used by Crusaders flying as flak suppressors, the weapons being loaded into tubes attached to three of the four missile "Y" racks bolted to the fuselage sides forward of the wing. This F-8E from VF-53 is being loaded with 45lb Zunis (which could be fitted with fragmentation, anti-armor, or smoke warheads) whilst chained down over *Ticonderoga*'s bow catapult one. (US Navy)

Some squadrons, notably VF-211, for part of 1967 loaded AIM-9Cs for head-on night attacks, where the weapon's radar seeker could work without an infrared target. For the May 19, 1967 mission that resulted in four MiG kills (two apiece for VF-24 and VF-22), the F-8E of Cdr Paul Speer had two AIM-9Cs on its port missile rails and two AIM-9Ds on the right side. However, the more complex AIM-9C, developed specifically for the F-8 to give it all-weather missile capability, was seldom used and scored no aerial kills.

IR versions of the AIM-9 had simple electronics and a fairly robust structure – factors which contributed to their overall success in destroying a target in every 5.5 launches, compared with one in 11 for the far more complex radar-guided AIM-7E Sparrow III. Sidewinders were the most successful air-to-air weapons in Vietnam, with a total of 80 kills, compared with 52 for Sparrows and 47 by gunfire.

For Crusader units, Sidewinders boosted their success rate to 0.72 kills per engagement – 19 kills in 25 MiG engagements between 1966 and 1968. Over a similar period, US F-4 Phantom II units destroyed 12 MiGs in 39 engagements (0.30 per fight). Later, improved tactics, better missiles, and more logical rules of engagement enabled US Navy and US Marine Corps Phantom II crews to down 26 MiGs, including nine MiG-21s, when combat over North Vietnam resumed in 1972. All but two were scored with AIM-9s. By then, only four squadrons were still flying F-8s on WestPac deployments. In the final analysis, all US Navy versus MiG encounters resulted in a kill ratio of 3.5 victories for each loss. In that context, the F-8's six-to-one ratio was exceptional.

In practice, a Crusader pilot fighting over North Vietnam depended upon offshore controllers such as *Red Crown* to vector him towards threats, rather than relying on his own extremely limited radar. In mid-1968, six out of seven MiG engagements involving F-8s were controlled by *Red Crown*.

The Crusader's radar was more useful for finding tankers or joining up with a strike package. Once in the general vicinity of a contact, it was up to the pilot to acquire it visually.

The Opposition

A development of the 1947-vintage MiG-15, the MiG-17F was also a point-defense interceptor. Its longer rear fuselage housed a simple afterburner for the VK-1F engine, giving a maximum thrust of 7,450lbs compared with 18,000lbs for the F-8E's J57-P-20. A fully loaded MiG-17 weighed in at 13,386lbs, while an F-8E reached 29,000lbs. The E-model Crusader's extra power compensated for its reduced maneuverability at 350–400 knots compared with the smaller MiG, while its maximum speed of 1,225mph at 36,000ft was almost twice that of the MiG-17. However, most aerial combat took place at much lower speeds and altitudes, where the F-8's better acceleration and far superior rate of climb gave US Navy pilots a clear advantage over their VPAF opponents. Unlike the J57-P-20, the VK-1F was slow to accelerate and its afterburner took more than five seconds to activate.

Structurally, the MiG-17 was simple and quite rugged, with no vulnerable wing fuel tanks and very basic maintenance requirements. Like the MiG-21, it had poor forward visibility due to a thick, bulletproof windscreen and a large ASP-4NM gunsight that was very susceptible to vibration. The ability to perform tight turns was the strong suit of both types, and the MiG-21's small size and smokeless exhaust made it hard to detect either visually or on radar. Armed with one unusually heavy-caliber, slow-firing Nudel'man N-37D 37mm cannon and two Nudel'man-Rikhter NR-23 23mm weapons, the MiG-17 suffered from poor gun harmonization and an inaccurate gunsight. Nevertheless, one 37mm shell could cause heavy damage, although only 40 were carried, with 80 for each 23mm gun.

The MiG-17's impressive maneuverability, due mainly to its very low wing loading of 44–47lb ft², gave it an advantage over virtually all US fighters in a close dogfight, including the F-8, for which comparable figures were 69–75lb ft². At high speeds, it had less of a turning advantage over the Crusader, as its flight controls became heavy and less effective. The delta-winged, Mach 2-capable MiG-21 had a wing loading of 65–70lb ft², giving it less maneuverability as a trade-off against supersonic speed. The jet also suffered from severe buffeting at lower altitudes when it exceeded Mach 0.92. The MiG-21's Mach 2 performance was only possible at high altitude, where it compared favorably with the F-8. At 15,000ft, where the jet was still a match for an F-8, it was limited to a speed of 595 knots. Like the Crusader, the MiG-21 had an impressive rate of climb.

After Bellinger's MiG-21 victory, F-8 pilots claimed three more without loss by mid-September 1968. Their early fights with the aircraft showed them that the MiG-21 was a high-speed "slash-and-dash" interceptor, and less threatening at lower speeds and altitudes. It relied on AIM-9B Sidewinder-copy R-3S "Atoll" missiles rather than cannon. The "Atoll's" faster-burning rocket motor gave it a higher speed than the AIM-9B, but a shorter effective range of around 7,000–8,000ft. The VPAF's early MiG-21F-13 "Fishbed C" was integrally

fitted with a single Nudel'man-Rikhter NR-30 30mm cannon with 60 rounds, but guns were deleted from the MiG-21PFL and MiG-21PFM – the latter variant had the option of carrying a twin-barrel Gryasev-Shipunov GSh-23 23mm cannon in a centerline pod.

US Navy pilots learned MiG-21 tactics following clashes with the fighter in 1966, observing their three- or four-ship flights spread out in line-astern. They saw that the first jet was used to distract an opposing fighter formation, leaving the trailing two MiGs to strike from high and behind at superior speed. Most US fighters' poor rearward visibility facilitated these attacks, although the MiG-21 itself had a blind "cone" extending 40 degrees on either side of the tail. Its tight canopy and armor plating restricted the pilot's head movements, and the low seat position limited sideways visibility to 20 degrees above the horizon.

Have Drill and *Have Doughnut* (USAF/US Navy trial combats with a captured MiG-17 and MiG-21 acquired from Israel) compared the fighters directly. Jerry Houston was one of the pilots involved in the evaluation, noting that "during *Have Drill*, none of the Navy's participating fighter pilots, whether in F-4s or F-8s, ever beat a MiG-17 one-versus-one." *Have Doughnut* showed that the F-8 and MiG-21 were closely matched, although the MiG's lower wing loading made it slightly more maneuverable below 400 knots. Crusaders were more stable, 150 knots faster at lower altitudes, and possessed a superior roll rate. A MiG-21 pilot had great difficulty in evading a Crusader if it got on his tail. An F-8's best rate of turn ("corner velocity") was at around 375 knots, with the pilot using the rudder and avoiding use of the ailerons.

A camouflaged MiG-17F of the 923rd FR shares the flightline at Gia Lam with a MiG-21U "Mongol-B" trainer and four MiG-21F-13s from the 921st FR in August 1966. "Red bandits" from the 923rd were frequently encountered by F-8 units in the skies over North Vietnam in 1966–68. (István Toperczer Collection)

CHAPTER 5
ART OF WAR

Most F-8 squadrons' missions were for various types of combat air patrols (CAPs). For VF-211 embarked in *Bon Homme Richard* in 1967, CAPs comprised more than 60 percent of the sorties flown, while the next most common, armed reconnaissance, occupied only 12 percent. The top CAP priority was usually barrier air combat patrols (BARCAPs), involving patrols to block bomb-carrying MiGs that threatened US naval forces operating up to 150 miles offshore in the Gulf of Tonkin – beyond the ships' own Talos SAM engagement zone. MiG interception of offshore US reconnaissance and radar picket aircraft was also a threat that had to be dealt with by F-8s on BARCAP.

Other variations on CAP duty included TARCAP, for which fighters (usually one division) closely escorted strike forces to and from a target, and FORCECAP, which was a variation on BARCAP, but with a range of controlling radar ships that varied daily. In addition, many missions were directed over the Ho Chi Minh Trail's Operation *Steel Tiger* areas against enemy transport heading into South Vietnam from Laos and Cambodia.

A fighter division consisted of four jets flying in two sections, each typically with a senior officer leader and a junior officer wingman. In this formation (officially known as a "combat spread" or "tactical wing") all pilots weaved to watch for rear attacks, compensating for the F-8's poor rearward visibility. MiGCAP tasked them with engaging enemy fighters which attempted to intercept strike groups. For MiGCAP missions, two or four AIM-9Ds were carried and a section of F-8s was assigned to the strike aircraft.

Controlled by an offshore strike support ship, the MiGCAP orbited "feet wet" (over the Gulf of Tonkin and parallel to the coastline) at around 20,000–25,000ft. If MiGs threatened the strikers, the shipboard fighter controller (*Red Crown*) would vector Crusaders towards the threat, positioning them within gun range around 1,000ft behind a target. A second section could be vectored towards the MiGs, staying three or four miles behind the lead section, from where the F-8s could make high-speed slashing attacks.

Crusader sections entered the target area at around 600 knots, maintaining low altitudes of 1,000–1,500ft to stay below enemy radar and doing their best to avoid known flak or SAM sites. They flew about one to two miles abeam each other so that either pilot could make a full radius turn and maneuver to check for threats behind his partner. The "shooter" F-8 could be either aircraft, which meant that "lead" could be quickly passed between the pilots, giving either one the opportunity to take advantage of a favorable attack position. One pilot would usually climb slightly above a partner who was in a good shooting position so that he could dive and chase off any other fighters who approached the shooter. If the lead F-8 turned to follow a MiG, but the MiG turned too tightly, his wingman could then turn more sharply from behind to cut the enemy fighter off. A four-aircraft division usually split into two elements if combat began.

Additionally, fighters undertook flak suppression and weather reconnaissance, and also provided escorts for dedicated photo-reconnaissance aircraft like RF-8As. Weather "recce" flights were often combined with armed reconnaissance against coastal targets of opportunity, which saw the Crusaders carrying LAU-10 rocket launchers or Mk 82 500lb bombs.

Of all these assignments, BARCAP was noted for its general tedium, although in the rare moments of action more than 60 percent of US aerial victories were scored during BARCAP and TARCAP (escort nearer or over the target) sorties. Launching first from the carrier, ahead of an Alpha strike package, a BARCAP F-8 section would fly to the "on station" position off the North Vietnamese coast. In daylight conditions, they flew racetrack patterns, with two F-8s in "loose deuce" formation under radar control and radio communication via UHF (281.9 MHz) from the *Red Crown* destroyer or cruiser stationed offshore.

Mutual support within a section, or "loose deuce," was a basic tenet of the US Navy's combat tactics. Lt Cdrs Jerry Houston and John Nichols, who were both tactics instructors with VF-124 at the time, were selected to review the NATOPS (Naval Air Training and Operating Procedures Standardization) classified manual in Dallas, Texas, in late 1968, "paying particular attention to the loose deuce maneuvering section. Almost nothing that I can recall needed changing," Jerry noted. "Keeping the wingman's 'six o'clock' clear, and mutual support when engaged, hadn't changed much since World War II, regardless of fighter type. That was prior to *Have Drill* and *Have Doughnut*. Those two highly secret at the time programs afforded more precise tactical maneuvering guidance, especially against the MiG-17, the result of which was that we never lost another fighter to that aircraft."

At night, a separation of two to five miles was maintained between aircraft, which flew in "trail" formation and with onboard radar contact between them. If one aircraft's radar failed, the section closed in together. Sending aloft a replacement BARCAP division usually began the sequence of launching the strike group. Having the fighters in the air first meant that the new CAPs were in place as the group (usually 16 A-4s and four F-8s) approached the target area at 22,000ft. The strike group was also supported by a Shrike-toting A-4 *Iron Hand* section together with its F-8 escorts, F-8 flak suppressors, and an F-8 TARCAP section. Crusaders escorted the *Iron Hand* A-4s to their launch point, and followed up a Shrike hit with 20mm gunfire against the missile site.

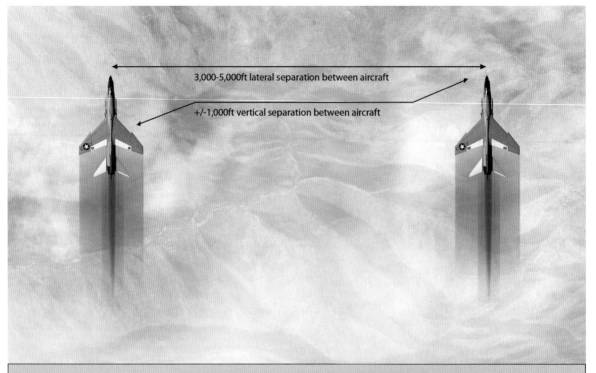

3,000-5,000ft lateral separation between aircraft

+/-1,000ft vertical separation between aircraft

F-8 CRUSADER TACTICAL FORMATION

In "loose deuce," as depicted here, both pilots watched for threats behind each other and closed in on any that appeared. Given the unreliability of the F-8's radar, the Tactical Lead pilot was usually the one with the functioning system while his wingman resorted to performing a visual-only search for VPAF fighters.

Often, the section had to split up and enter individual dogfights, but with the risk of getting "jumped" by an unseen intruder. The NAVAIR F-8 Tactical Manual stated that "unit integrity" in loose deuce "means three things: A) knowing the position of your teammate at all times. B) maintaining a position advantageous to his defense. C) maintaining team offensive potential." "In practice," as MiG killer Phil Vampatella recalled, "loose deuce was great, but in reality in my experience it soon went right down the toilet once enemy fighters were spotted."

Equally as hazardous as dueling with well-defended SAM sites were flak suppression missions in which pilots had to detect and shoot at AAA positions with rockets and 20mm gunfire from close quarters to draw enemy fire away from strike aircraft. Their success in this role is indicated by the fact that only four F-8s were lost during the course of these missions. Flak suppression was not an obvious task for the F-8, which lacked a serviceable bombsight or substantial ordnance capacity, and relied on rockets rather than the more effective Rockeye cluster bomb units used by F-4s undertaking such missions. Crusader pilots were often given a specific gun to hit, based on recent reconnaissance pictures. Their effect tended to be psychological in reducing rather than defeating the AAA opposing strike aircraft.

In 1967, VF-162's CO, Cdr Charles "Cal" Swanson, wanted his squadron (part of CVW-16, embarked in *Oriskany*) to spend more time flying as bombers

rather than undertaking so many unproductive BARCAP missions. Bombing had occupied a smaller proportion of the F-8 squadrons' time when Alpha strikes were increased in 1965–66, but for squadrons on *Dixie Station*, ground attack was a daily occupation. Some of Dick Schaffert's early missions with VF-111 involved dropping napalm on poorly defined targets in the Mekong Delta under the guidance of a USAF forward air controller.

North Vietnam had only a limited number of MiGs in the early war years, which meant that they were used sparingly. The VPAF's GCI looked for weaknesses in US attack formations and directed fighters towards situations where they might have a clear advantage. Although MiG encounters were uncommon, engagements could develop into epic dogfights like those seen in July 1967. They could vary in length from 35 seconds in the case of Lt Cdr Nichols' fight, to ten minutes for Lt Cdr Schaffert's prolonged duel.

Crusader pilots, also reliant upon GCI guidance, felt that the VPAF avoided combat with them. During Alpha strikes, MiGs tended to remain in orbit

Shark-mouthed F-8D BuNo 148697 was used by VF-111 during its first war cruise – a long deployment with CVW-2 from March to November 1965 aboard *Midway*. The unit had initially been led by Cdr James D. La Haye until May 8, when he was shot down and killed during the attack on Vinh airfield; the US Navy's very first strike against a VPAF base. This aircraft's mixed AIM-9B and Zuni weapons load reflects the ground attack role predominantly undertaken by VF-111 on that cruise. (US Navy)

VF-111 avoided being tasked with bombing missions during its 1967–68 cruise with CVW-16 on board *Oriskany* simply because its veteran F-8Cs lacked underwing pylons. This meant sister-squadron VF-162 had to shoulder the ground attack burden with its F-8Es. Kept busy flying CAP missions, VF-111 had flown 1,617 combat sorties by early October 1967 – when it was still only halfway through the cruise. Amongst the pilots in this photograph are squadron CO Cdr Bob Rasmussen (standing, far left) and Lt Cdr Dick Schaffert (kneeling, far left), who survived a fiercely fought clash with multiple MiG-17s on December 14, 1967. (US Navy)

northwest of Hanoi, but flights of four fighters were sometimes sent against a strike group. A second flight might then be vectored in from a different direction and lower altitude in order to catch US aircraft from behind while the TARCAP was tackling the initial MiGs.

Alpha Strike Crusaders

A strike group for missions against North Vietnam comprised up to 30 aircraft, with supporting A-4 and KA-3 tankers. At 50 miles offshore, the armament switches were activated and the group descended to 12,000–14,000ft, from where the bombers would begin their roll-in to attack the target. The faster F-8s weaved to keep their speed down as they followed the strikers at around 350 knots, looking out for MiGs and SAMs. *Iron Hand* A-4s with Shrike anti-radiation missiles, plus F-8 escorts, then detached to attack pre-arranged SAM sites.

Iron Hand aircraft were prime targets for enemy interceptors, and their F-8 escorts could warn them of threats from the ground and direct CAP Crusaders towards any aerial intruders or tackle the MiGs by themselves. Aside from issuing SAM and MiG warnings, F-8 pilots worked in radio silence, communicating by encrypted codes or hand-signals to indicate course changes, armament states or fuel levels. At the same time, the flak suppressors flew ahead and selected the most active AAA sites to attack with 20mm and Zunis a minute or two before the bombers began their attack runs. Since the latter had to drop their ordnance at low altitudes, their escorts also had to fly at similar altitudes, thus reducing their turning space and impeding their ability to engage MiGs.

Pilots tried to prioritize a quick attack rather than being drawn into a turning fight where MiG-17s had the advantage. However, as Jerry Houston pointed out, "Between 500–550 knots, the MiG-17's turn capability [aileron control] diminished severely. The control stick almost became unmovable to the left or right – quite a handicap."

Strike aircraft pulled out of their dives at no lower than 3,000ft, at which point F-8 pilots usually lit their afterburners to regain altitude and avoid AAA. They then tried to regroup in sections on deliberately unpredictable courses to the coast, the whole attack having taken around three minutes. When Crusader pilots engaged MiGs chasing the bombers, the resulting combats mostly occurred below 10,000ft at subsonic speeds, and MiG pilots often began the engagement with a height advantage.

Upon returning to the carrier, a new cycle would begin for the launch of another Alpha strike. An Essex-class carrier assigned

Alpha strikes were large-scale coordinated attacks, usually by aircraft from two carrier air wings. Here, Crusaders and Skyhawks from CVW-21 await unchaining and then direction to catapults prior to the start of an Alpha strike from *Hancock* in the early spring of 1965. Aside from the Zuni- and Sidewinder-armed F-8Es from VF-24 and VF-211 crowding the stern of the carrier, there is also a solitary RF-8A from VFP-63 Det L chained to the flightdeck third from the right. Its pilot would be charged with capturing post-attack photographs of the target shortly after the Alpha strike had cleared the area. (Peter Mersky Collection)

to *Yankee Station*, 90 miles east of the North Vietnamese coast, would expect to launch and recover two or three such strikes daily during its 12-hour operational window before the tasking was passed to another carrier on the mission schedule issued by TF 77. During *Rolling Thunder*, the launch sequences would include night strike packages.

Iron Hand escort sorties were usually the least popular among F-8 pilots because of the fairly low speeds and altitudes they had to observe in order to stay with the attacking Skyhawks. Flying "low and slow" made the Crusaders both "flak magnets" and SAM targets, just like the Shrike-launcher A-4s that were particularly disliked by enemy defenders. Jets flying *Iron Hand* escort were also less likely to be presented with MiG-killing opportunities, which Crusader pilots saw as their primary role. In tactics pioneered by Cdr Dick Bellinger of VF-162, a section of lightly armed F-8s preceded the strike force to attract SAMs that might otherwise be launched at the bombers. Without the encumbrance of underwing loads, the Crusader pilots had a better chance to out-maneuver the Mach 2.5 SAMs or drop chaff bundles to divert them.

Solo MiGs often appeared up to 40 miles from the strike package's known direction, hoping to lure the MiGCAP F-8s away in a tail chase or force them to fly over heavy AAA and SAM concentrations. Feint attacks on the formation had a similar aim. Although most BARCAPs were uneventful, both *Red Crown* and the pilots maintained constant vigilance. Several MiG kills were achieved during BARCAPs and VPAF fighters were chased away on numerous occasions. The BARCAP was seldom diverted towards over-land engagements, but it occasionally escorted USAF operations such as RC-135M "Combat Apple" aircraft on communications and electronic intelligence gathering missions.

BARCAP fighters had their tanks topped up halfway through their patrol cycle by A-4 Skyhawks equipped with "buddy pack" refueling gear, the jets being capable of passing 1,500lbs of fuel to each F-8. Patrol times could be shortened if tankers were unavailable, or extended to a "double cycle" if the relief F-8 section was unable to take over the CAP. Crusader pilots would have a complete top-up of liquid oxygen in case this occurred. A-3 Skywarrior tankers were also available, these typically being used to meet aircraft returning from strikes and needing the bigger tanker's extra fuel capacity. Their pilots routinely banked to raise a wing towards approaching "clients" – an invitation signal that was visible many miles away.

Tankers were crucial for all strike aircraft, and particularly for jets with afterburning engines which often approached fuel starvation. On September 17, 1968, Lt(jg) Paul Swigart of VF-24, flying from *Hancock*, was involved in an indecisive eight-minute duel with two MiG-21s in which he remained in afterburner for too long. The engine of his F-8H flamed out before he could reach a tanker and Swigert ejected near the island of Hon Nieu, off the North

In-flight refueling was essential for all carrier-based Crusader units during the Vietnam War. Here, an A-4E "Tinker Tanker" refuels an F-8J from VF-211 during a mission from *Hancock* in the summer of 1973. Occasionally, a refueling "basket" and hose was ingested by an F-8's intake, requiring speed reduction by both tanker and Crusader to allow the Skyhawk, Skywarrior, or Corsair II to pull it out. (US Navy)

Vietnamese coast. He was rescued by a search-and-rescue helicopter. Swigert was subsequently killed on February 4, 1969 in a ramp strike at the end of a CAP mission.

One of the escorts' main problems was that the North Vietnamese invariably had ample advance notice of their approach from early-warning radar stations and the numerous vessels offshore posing as fishing boats. MiGs could easily take off, patrol at low altitudes below US radar and then climb to attack an incoming strike force from behind and below.

US Navy pilots believed that the VPAF's GCI would only commit MiGs to an interception if they thought they had the tactical advantage. They would withdraw the fighters if this was lost. F-8 pilots, therefore, tried to move between the MiGs and their bases to cut them off from retreat and compel them to fight. They would descend to very low altitudes to evade North Vietnamese early warning radars and await guidance from *Red Crown* and from their own radars. If a division leader spotted the "bandits" first, he would lead the attack or pass the lead to a wingman who had also seen the enemy. Speeds above 450 knots were recommended on patrol so that pilots could react to a threat quickly.

Engagements would ideally begin with a near-supersonic attack into the MiG's blind spot, similar to the tactics used by MiG-21 pilots, with isolated single VPAF fighters becoming primary targets. Pilots positioned themselves around 3,000–5,000ft behind the enemy to move in for a missile or gun attack. If the attacker overshot his slower target, a high-G barrel roll or a "yo-yo" – a rapid climb and descent while following the enemy in a turn – prevented the target aircraft from getting behind the Crusader. A "scissors" maneuver, in either the vertical or horizontal plane, was a series of weaving, spiraling reverse turns to keep the attacking fighter from overshooting his target. If the opponent was a MiG-21, US Navy pilots were told to try and force the engagement down below 16,000ft, where the MiG's reduced rate of roll, acceleration, and control "heaviness" could be exploited.

F-8 and F-4 pilots were instructed to maintain high energy during an engagement and avoid slow-speed maneuvering fights. As Crusader pilot Lt(jg) Chuck Rice commented, it takes "a heck of a lot of afterburner" for a loaded F-8 to catch up with a division once it "got slow." They were encouraged to use their vertical acceleration to outdistance MiGs and re-position for an attack. As one Crusader instructor put it, "fast and vertical is the F-8's game."

Although five US Marine Corps squadrons saw combat in Southeast Asia with the Crusader, only VMF(AW)-212 did so from a carrier flightdeck. The vast majority of the unit's flying whilst embarked in *Oriskany* as part of CVW-16 took the form of close air support missions, with VMF(AW)-212 completing 1,588 combat sorties. Two of the squadron's three F-8Es seen here chained down to the flightdeck alongside Crusaders from VF-162 have significant cordite residue around their gun ports. (US Navy)

A high state of situational awareness was required to detect other MiGs waiting to "jump" the F-8s from the rear as they headed for a threat. By 1967, VPAF controllers were using MiG-21s to lure escort fighters away from the strike group. They would then send MiG-17s in from other directions at very low altitudes to attack the strikers.

Red Crown and other control sources were crucial when it came to a successful interception. For an optimum engagement, the CAP fighters had to be positioned less than three miles behind the MiGs, while also keeping them clear of the immediate target area. A second CAP section would ideally be vectored to a position around five miles behind the first to catch any MiGs attacking from the rear. F-8 pilots had to be given enough distance to complete an interception before the MiGs escaped to safe sanctuary. Controllers also had to manage the provision of tankers for the CAP and, where possible, additional fighters to protect a CAP as it egressed, short of fuel and ammunition – the ideal situation for MiG pilots in pursuit.

Although MiG encounters were fairly rare for F-8 pilots, the VPAF and the Chinese People's Liberation Army Air Force (PLAAF) caused 16 aircraft from the US Navy and US Marine Corps to be lost during the war – 3.3 percent of the 473 aircraft lost over North Vietnam. Three were F-8Es, shot down between June and September 1966.

Throughout the conflict, no US Navy strike packages were forced to turn back because of MiG opposition. Nevertheless, they caused considerable disruption to many strikes, making numerous bombers jettison their loads and maneuver defensively. The constant requirement for CAPs placed great demands upon all carrier air wing fighters. The MiG threat could undoubtedly have been reduced by attacks on their bases, but politicians in Washington, D.C. ruled these out until April 1967, by which time MiGs had shot down 25 US aircraft. Other airfield attacks followed in the last two months of 1967, and the VPAF responded by moving its aircraft temporarily to PLAAF bases in China.

During most photo-reconnaissance missions flown by RF-8A/Gs from Essex-class carriers, Crusaders provided their fighter escort due to their similar performance making them an ideal pairing. They proceeded towards the coast at 15,000–20,000ft, usually without CAP support, crossing the target area at 5,000–6,000ft, with the escort F-8 pilot looking out for ground fire or

Lt Col Charles Ludden, CO of VMF(AW)-212, became the first US Marine Corps officer to command a carrier air wing (albeit in a temporary capacity for just 25 days) following the shooting down of Cdr James Stockdale on September 9, 1965. He would retain this unique distinction until January 2006, when Col D. P. Yurovich assumed command of CVW-9. (US Navy)

hostile fighters. Tanking was usually provided shortly after going "feet wet" to top up the aircraft after their fuel-gobbling high-speed, low altitude run.

The first US Navy aircraft to be lost in Southeast Asia was the unescorted RF-8A flown by Lt Charles Klusmann from VFP-63 Det C, embarked in *Kitty Hawk*, on June 6, 1964. When his aircraft was hit by 37mm ground fire during a *Yankee Team* flight over Laos, Klusmann became the first pilot to eject from a Crusader in combat. The success of escorted (either by F-4s or F-8s) reconnaissance missions was demonstrated by the fact that VPAF MiGs failed to shoot down a single protected RF-8. Pilots were allocated photo escort on a rota basis but, as Phil Vampatella, recalled, "it was a God-awful mission and we hated it. There wasn't a whole lot we could do [on that mission] except follow him, and we didn't have any autonomy. It just felt like we were going into danger for no reason." Photo escort missions comprised a substantial part of the F-8 squadrons' operational tasking after the 1968 bombing halt.

Crusader pilots prioritized gun attacks using tail-chase pursuit at close quarters or deflection shooting. In so doing, they could also place their fighters within the relatively narrow "cone" in which an AIM-9 Sidewinder could detect a hot target and home successfully. Thoroughly familiar with close, maneuvering combat in order to bring their weapons to bear on a target, F-8 pilots routinely used their gunnery skills in Vietnam. VF-191 alone expended 23,000 rounds of 20mm ammunition, in addition to 300 Zuni rockets and 100 tons of bombs, in more than 1,000 combat sorties flown from *Ticonderoga* between October 1966 and May 1967 – the unit also lost two aircraft and two pilots during this deployment. VF-191 made eight war cruises with CVW-19 in just nine years.

The 20 US Marine Corps squadrons that flew F-8s were mostly trained in fighter tactics, although almost all of their combat experience was gained flying in close air support missions over South Vietnam. This also applied to Lt Col Charles Ludden's VMF(AW)-212, which was the first and only US Marine Corps F-8 squadron to undertake a combat deployment embarked in a US Navy carrier. Part of CVW-16 on board *Oriskany* between April and December 1965, it had transitioned from F-8Ds to F-8Es prior to deployment so as to operate identical equipment to sister-squadron VF-162 during the cruise. Whilst assigned to TF 77, VMF(AW)-212 completed 1,588 combat sorties.

When the CO of CVW-16, Cdr James Stockdale, was shot down and captured on September 9, 1965, Ludden became the first US Marine Corps officer to command a carrier air wing. Like other "Flying Leatherneck" F-8 pilots, Ludden's "jocks" were keen to fight MiGs but never had the opportunity to claim an aerial victory. The unit lost four Crusaders on deployment, two in combat (with one pilot captured and the other rescued) and two in operational accidents (both pilots recovered).

MiGs And Other Hazards

The first 32 MiG-17s for the VPAF arrived at the newly constructed air base at Noi Bai (Phuc Yen), near Hanoi, in August 1964 for the 921st FR, their pilots having been trained by Soviet instructors at the four airfields used by the Krasnodar Flight Officers' School between the Black Sea and Azov Sea. Pilots had also began training there on the more challenging MiG-21 in early 1962. Many trainees found that their smaller stature and poor fitness meant that they could not handle the faster MiG-21, which entered operational service with the VPAF in January 1966. Pilots had difficulty in seeing out of the already cluttered windscreen, in reaching the rudder pedals and in withstanding G-loads when undertaking ACM training.

Until the Gulf of Tonkin incident in August 1964 initiated hostilities between North Vietnam and US Navy vessels, the 921st FR was temporarily based at Mengzi (Mong Tu) air base in southern China, where its pilots were continuing to be trained. On August 6 they moved to Noi Bai, although the "Silver Swallows" (MiG-17s) did not commence operational flying until April 3, 1965 in response to reprisal air strikes on North Vietnam by US aircraft in Operations *Flaming Dart* and *Rolling Thunder*. The following day, the 921st was credited with its first two victories when a pair of F-105D Thunderchiefs were shot down. On April 9, an F-4B of VF-96 (embarked in USS *Ranger* (CVA-61) as part of CVW-9) was shot down by MiG-17s (Shenyang-built J-5s) from the PLAAF.

Training continued as the MiG pilots learned to operate within the rigid Soviet-installed GCI system with its four main sites and up to 200 early-warning radars. Controllers managed every aspect of their flights, vectoring them to their targets for interception from the most favorable position, and guiding them on their speed, timing, and use of armament. They warned them of US fighters, with exact instructions on when to break off an engagement.

By mid-1972, MiG tactics had settled into a pattern whereby a flight of two MiG-21s and a pair of MiG-17s launched from bases such as Bai Thuong and headed south at around 8,000ft. The MiG-17s were then vectored towards incoming US Navy aircraft and engaged them. The MiG-21 section, meanwhile, was orbiting some distance away at a lower altitude, from which it would climb beneath the US Navy force, make a single attack with "Atoll" missiles at high speed, and then withdraw to safety.

The main threat to US Marine Corps F-8s, which seldom encountered MiGs, was groundfire, which accounted for 94 percent of losses to known causes. An equivalent US Navy figure was 77 percent. Essex-class carrier air wings launched sections of F-8s armed with Zuni rockets and 20mm guns to attack AAA sites ahead of strikes, firing at the most visible sources of gunfire

flashes. Combined with SAMs, AAA was the most frequent cause of F-8 losses.

On its 1965–66 cruise embarked in *Bon Homme Richard* as part of CVW-19, VF-191 lost four of its 12 F-8Es in four months to AAA and SAMs (with one pilot killed, two captured, and one rescued), while its sister-squadron VF-194 had three jets downed by AAA (three pilots recovered). Adding three operational losses (in which two pilots were killed) in landing or take-off crashes and one RF-8A downed by AAA (its pilot was also

Storeless F-8J BuNo 150904 from VF-191 is waved off after attempting to land on board *Oriskany* during the carrier's fourth war cruise in 1969. An arrested landing often threw the entire weight of the aircraft onto the nose-gear trunnion as the main landing gear wheels left the deck for a second. The distance from the edge of the stern ramp to the first arresting wire on the flightdeck of a SCB-27C Essex-class carrier was a mere 90ft, compared with 170ft on later, larger carriers like Nimitz-class vessels, requiring extreme precision by the pilot on approach. (US Navy)

killed) brings the total of lost Crusaders to 11 in one carrier air wing in five months. Four of the aircraft were downed by AAA in 11 days during the carrier's final On Line Period in November, with one of those lost being the CO of VF-191, Cdr H. E. "Howie" Rutledge. A 200-mission veteran of the Korean War, Rutledge spent the next seven years as a PoW.

Flying straight and level over key targets, and sometimes having to repeat a photo run, meant that RF-8 pilots flew the most consistently hazardous Crusader missions – their loss rates were three times the average for US Navy aircraft. Aside from a single deployment by VFP-62's Det 42, VFP-63's various detachments undertook the RF-8 photo-reconnaissance tasking throughout the war. This in turn meant that its aircraft comprised 25 percent of all Crusader losses in Southeast Asia.

SA-2 SAMs were a threat to all F-8 activity, even BARCAP missions that were usually flown offshore. CVW-16's first SAM loss, on October 5, 1965, was the F-8E of VF-162 pilot Lt(jg) Rick Adams, who was flying as wingman to Cdr Dick Bellinger as the pair crossed the coast at 30,000ft while protecting a strike on a bridge at Kep. The missile detonated just behind Adams' Crusader, starting a fire which eventually made the aircraft explode after it had struggled 40 miles out to sea. He ejected and was rescued, only to be shot down again by AAA on July 12, 1966 while trying to evade another SAM – again, Adams was rescued. His first shootdown was an example of a familiar problem for F-8 pilots. Bellinger had attempted to warn him of two SA-2s that had been launched in their direction, but Adams did not hear him. Radio problems were behind many losses to MiGs and other hazards during the conflict in Vietnam.

Lt Anthony Moore of VF-191 was flying a BARCAP at 33,000ft 40 miles off Hanoi on October 27, 1965 when an SA-2 burst through the undercast and blew the tail off his F-8E, consigning him to eight years in prison. Another early SAM loss was Lt Terry Dennison from VF-162, whose F-8E was struck by an SA-2 at 12,000ft without any warning during a July 19, 1966 strike on the Co Trai bridge. No fewer than 13 SA-2s were fired at US Navy aircraft during this mission. It is believed that Dennison died in captivity.

CHAPTER 6
COMBAT

Until June 1966, Crusader pilots had only glimpsed MiGs from afar, aside from one brief encounter on April 3, 1965 when a MiG-17 flight made a single firing pass on an Alpha strike force, badly damaging Lt Cdr Spence Thomas' VF-211 F-8E. The VPAF credited the pilots involved with shooting the Crusader down, although as previously noted, the jet landed at Da Nang. The following day, the 921st FR shot down two USAF F-105s.

Cdr Jack Monger, commanding CVW-21 during *Hancock*'s second combat cruise (November 1965 to August 1966), resolved to enable his Crusader pilots (in VF-211, again flying F-8Es, and in VF-24, equipped with F-8Cs) to grapple with the VPAF so that they could claim the fighter's first aerial victories. In order to do this, he integrated the F-8 escort more closely into CVW-21's Alpha strike group, which was where MiG pilots concentrated their attention. VF-211's CO, Cdr Harold "Hal" Marr, was keen to comply, and he led a small Alpha strike of A-4s from *Hancock* at noon on June 12 against barracks in Haiphong. Lt(jg) Phil Vampatella was his wingman (in "Nickel 110"), while a section of F-8Cs from VF-24 (call-sign "Page Boy") led by Lt Fred Richardson, with Lt(jg) Denis Duffy as his wingman, completed the division.

They approached the target at 1,500ft, egressing along a narrow valley under cloud. Vampatella, on Marr's wing (and noted for his great eyesight), saw two aircraft a mile behind them at 2,000ft. As Vampatella explained:

We worked on the basis that "he who sees, leads." Whoever sees the enemy first becomes the flight leader. I led the break into the MiGs, and from that point on during the

VF-211 CO Cdr "Hal" Marr safes his ejection seat with help from his plane captain upon returning to *Hancock* from his MiG-killing sortie in F-8E BuNo 150924 on June 12, 1966. Marr was a veteran fighter pilot (with more than 1,500 hours in the F-8) by the time he claimed the Crusader's first aerial success. Subsequently transferred to VF-162, BuNo 150924 was lost due to fuel starvation during a photo-escort mission from *Oriskany* on October 6, 1966. (Peter Mersky Collection)

entire flight I never saw another American airplane. Marr lost me, and it was a solo flight after the first break. I had two missiles. I fired the first one head-on, out of the envelope and with no chance of success, but I was anxious, young and scared. It didn't track and went stupid. I did some more turning and jinking and got on the tail of one of the MiGs. I was in range and I fired the second missile, but it did not leave the airplane. That happened way too often. A guy then passed right in front of me as an easier target, so I rolled in on him and fired my guns. They misfired after six or seven rounds. I gave up in disgust.

Reflecting on that encounter, Vampatella commented:

We did not maintain section integrity. That was one of the flaws of that time. The thinking then was that there would not be any dogfighting; we would just put a couple of missiles on these guys and intercept the enemy 200 miles from New York and blow them out of the sky. That thinking went out the window when we did start dogfighting. I have since spoken to pilots at Topgun and explained that the reason they exist is that we were so poor at dogfighting, and we had to learn it all over again.

Upon returning to the carrier, Marr made a 600mph pass below flightdeck level, pulling up into a barrel roll. However, he "boltered" on landing after he forgot to lower his arrestor hook. Once out of the jet, he received an enthusiastic reception for claiming the Crusader's first kill(s). This early engagement was a victory for F-8 dogfighting tactics, but it highlighted problems with the jet's armament, particularly the use and reliability of Sidewinders. Although Marr's second AIM-9D destroyed a MiG-17, his first missile was selected at a range of 2,500ft on his armament control panel, but it was launched at an excessive "angle off" and failed to track.

After firing 30 rounds at a second MiG-17, which were seen to damage the fighter's right wing, his guns stopped due to an electrical fault and Marr had to break off – he was initially credited with having damaged the aircraft, although this was later upgraded, albeit unofficially, many years later to a victory. Lt(jg) Duffy's guns would not charge and Richardson fired two Sidewinders that missed. He had fired one as the MiG sought to escape, but it fell short. A second MiG section returned briefly, and Richardson fired at it as the jet entered cloud. Duffy fired an AIM-9 at the section's wingman, but it was launched without a tone. Only one out of eight AIM-9Ds had hit a target. Three of the four F-8s had also suffered gun deficiencies.

Vampatella had a second chance to down a MiG on June 21 during another "Nickel" flight mission by three VF-211 Crusaders (a fourth aborted before launch) led by the squadron executive officer, Lt Cdr Cole Black, in an escort for an A-4 strike package targeting a bridge near Kep airfield. An RF-8A from *Hancock* flown by VFP-63 Det L pilot Lt Leonard Eastman and escorted by Vampatella's roommate, Lt Dick Smith, was in the area and was shot down by AAA (although VPAF pilots Pham Thanh Chung and Nguyen Van Bay claimed it too).

Black immediately took his division down to provide rescue cover (RESCAP) at a risky 1,500–2,000ft altitude over the cloud-covered valley that Eastman had parachuted into. Having sighted the downed pilot's position, Black and his wingman, Lt Gene Chancy ("Nickel 101"), who was a former RF-8A pilot, took turns at orbiting over the site while Lt Dick Smith and Lt(jg) Vampatella went to top up from a KA-3 tanker, returning to relieve Black and Chancy. There was copious AAA in the area, around 40 miles from Hanoi. Vampatella ("Nickel 104") was hit by a 37mm shell, taking a massive chunk out of his right UHT and punching 80 shrapnel holes in the airframe.

Black and Chancy were then jumped by four silver 923rd FR MiG-17s that approached from almost head-on. Black called a MiG alert and Smith's section, which had flown less than 15 miles towards the tanker for a second refueling

1200 hrs, JUNE 12, 1966

NEAR DAI TAN BARRACKS

1 Cdr Hal Marr ("Nickel 103") and Lt(jg) Phil Vampatella ("Nickel 110") of VF-211 escort two flights of Skyhawks, with Lt Fred Richardson's VF-24 F-8C section to their right, at 5,000ft. The Skyhawks have bombed the Dai Tan barracks complex. They are heading for the coast.

2 Vampatella sees four MiG-17s approaching at very low altitude from the Crusaders' "seven o'clock" position ten miles behind them and in afterburner, leaving visible smoke trails.

3 The Crusaders pull a hard left 7g turn towards the oncoming MiGs, which are approaching in two pairs at 500 knots at an altitude of 2,000ft. The F-8s, in afterburner at 450 knots, meet the MiGs virtually head-on. The latter make a sharp 6g turn into the Crusaders and pass them. Marr briefly fires at one without visible results.

4 Marr and Vampatella perform a sharp right reverse turn in a "scissors" maneuver, passing two of the MiGs once again. The other MiG section splits off and attempts to flee.

5 The two MiGs that Marr and Vampatella are following also separate. Richardson and his wingman, Lt(jg) Denis Duffy, chase the leader (in an unpainted jet) while Marr and Vampatella follow the wingman (whose fighter is gray).

6 Marr and Vampatella make three horizontal left turns, after which "Nickel 103" performs a series of "high yo-yo" maneuvers to try and get behind the MiG. He opens fire with 90 degrees deflection, but misses his quarry.

7 Vampatella switches his attention to the leader of the break-away second MiG section, flying at 3,000ft. He triggers a Sidewinder from 3,700ft which "hangs up." His second missile goes ballistic. Spotting the wingman from the second section off to his left, "Nickel 110" then closes in behind the MiG but his guns jam. Vampatella gives up "in disgust" and heads for the coast.

8 With the silver MiG ahead of him, the "yo-yoing" Marr enters a valley in the mountains under low cloud. He fires a Sidewinder from 2,500ft which fails to guide and falls away.

9 Marr's MiG, low on fuel after prolonged afterburner use, stops maneuvering, goes wings level, and heads north. "Nickel 103" engages afterburner and, upon reaching a speed of 500 knots, fires his second Sidewinder. The missile cuts off the MiG's starboard wing and tail section. The VPAF fighter spins down into a small hamlet. No ejection is seen.

10 Marr, emerging from a solid bank of cloud, now sees the MiGs that Vampatella had been attacking. He climbs towards them, closing to within 600ft of the wingman, and opens firing with his four cannon. After only a few rounds, Marr's guns jam, but not before he has seen parts falling from the MiG's right wing. "Nickel 103" engages afterburner and returns to *Hancock*.

and was down to minimum fuel, immediately turned back into what soon became a violent dogfight.

Black turned at low altitude to get behind the intruders. Vampatella's damaged jet was hard to turn and slower than the F-8 flown by Smith. This meant that the latter accelerated ahead "on the deck" and faced two MiGs high and head-on. When he pulled up to fire at one, his guns jammed. Vampatella then spotted a MiG very close behind an F-8E just as it opened fire. "I didn't know which F-8 it was. Because of the damage to my airplane, I couldn't keep up with Dick Smith. I broadcast a warning for everybody to break, but unfortunately they didn't hear the warning." Phan Van Tu's shells hit Lt Cdr Black's Crusader seconds later. "I saw that MiG closing on him and then I saw the tail of his F-8 explode," Vampatella explained. Black ejected immediately. He was captured five minutes later, enduring almost seven years in captivity. Eastman was also caught shortly thereafter.

Lt Chancy, meanwhile, saw two MiGs ahead diving to attack him. He immediately fired 75 rounds at Duong Trung Tan's fighter as it passed at very close quarters. Parts of the aircraft's wing fell away and the MiG began trailing fuel. Duong Trung Tan then ejected. Chancy turned to pursue another MiG, diving in afterburner at low altitude and firing an AIM-9D at a range of 5,000ft as it climbed away. The MiG pilot turned sharply to evade the missile. Chancy then realized other MiGs were behind him, and one had opened fire with 37mm shells. He was in a low altitude turning fight, where the MiG had the advantage. Low on fuel, Chancy had to engage afterburner again and break away to find a tanker, before heading back to the carrier.

Another MiG followed Vampatella's Crusader, which was still sufficiently maneuverable to avoid the enemy jet's gunfire, and he headed for the tree-tops to shake off the pursuer. Engaging afterburner for several seconds, despite a low fuel state, Vampatella pulled ahead of the MiG in a slight climb. He then jinked violently, rolled inverted and dived at 600 knots from an altitude of 3,500ft. Vampatella recovered at tree-top level, later explaining, "I tried to scrape him off on the trees." A quick rearward check soon afterwards revealed the MiG pilot turning away for home.

Lt Gene Chancy in his assigned F-8E, "Nickel 108." His MiG kill was scored in BuNo 150910 "Nickel 101," Cdr "Hal" Marr's aircraft. Chancy ejected twice during his naval career – once during training and again on a May 2, 1966 strafing mission against an early warning radar installation on Hon Me Island. When AAA destroyed the hydraulic lines in his F-8E, he took to his parachute close to the island. Swimming hard against an incoming tide, Chancy was quickly picked up by a US Navy UH-2 Seasprite helicopter. (Peter Mersky Collection)

At that point the desire for retribution overcame Vampatella's awareness of his damaged aircraft and marginal fuel state. He turned back at maximum speed and caught up with the fleeing MiG. At around a mile he launched an AIM-9D, which guided well and "exploded to the right side of the MiG's tail. I never saw him crash or eject, but I heard that the pilot did eject and survive, which I was happy about."

He then turned once again towards the coast, calling urgently for a tanker despite his aircraft being hard to control, making refueling a challenging prospect. A buddy store-equipped A-4E from VA-212, flown by Lt Art Culver, responded, but all his disposable fuel in the store had been transferred. After some rapid calculations, Culver decided to transfer half his meager internal fuel to the buddy store, and from there to the starving Crusader. From Vampatella's perspective, "That was one of the most heroic things I have ever seen. I had five minutes of fuel left and I was still a long way from the carrier. We both had enough fuel for one shot at a carrier landing." Breaking the rules for a good "three-wire" landing, Vampatella caught the first wire (only the first and third were in place), as he knew he could not make a "go around" if he missed. He was awarded the Navy Cross for his exploits that day – the first fighter pilot in the war to receive one.

Lt(jg) Phil Vampatella relives his MiG-killing mission of June 21, 1966 in true fighter pilot fashion in VF-211's ready room on board *Hancock*. (US Navy)

Vampatella's F-8E was given a new UHT after it was put ashore in Japan, following which the aircraft was issued to VF-162 as an attrition replacement when *Oriskany* had a port call at Yokosuka in late July 1966. It did not last long with the unit, however, falling to AAA on August 18. Its pilot, Lt Cdr D. A. "Butch" Verich, was rescued. Eleven months later, on July 16, 1967, Verich was shot down again (and rescued) leading a flak suppression mission for A-4s attacking the marshaling yard at Phu Ly. His jet, hit by a SAM, was the third of eight combat losses suffered by CVW-16 during its first week on *Yankee Station* at the very start of *Oriskany*'s third war cruise. The carrier air wing would lose ten aircraft in total in July, and 29 during the whole cruise, eight of them being F-8C/Es to AAA and SAMs. Four more Crusaders were among CVW-16's ten operational losses. In total, three F-8 pilots were killed and two captured.

The MiG-17 kills credited to *Hancock*'s F-8 pilots during CVW-21's second war cruise were offset by eight combat losses of F-8C/E and RF-8A Crusaders to AAA and two more in accidents, resulting in four pilots being killed and three made PoWs. Nevertheless, Cdr Monger's more aggressive tactics when it came to dealing with the VPAF fighter threat had seen four MiGs shot down for the loss of two F-8s during 12 engagements in June–July 1966.

Anxious to add to the MiG kill tally after a luckless combat cruise embarked in *Oriskany* in 1965 as XO of VF-162, volatile but respected Cdr Dick "Belly" Bellinger (who had previously flown bombers with the USAAF in World War II) was now the CO of the unit. He had noticed that VPAF fighters habitually picked on the last flight of an Alpha strike package as it egressed. On July 14, 1966, Bellinger and his wingman, New Englander Lt Dick Wyman, along with Lt Chuck Tinker formed the "Superheat" CAP to follow the last A-4 divisions after they had targeted Nam Dinh, near Hanoi.

Posing as "extra Skyhawks" in an attempt to lure enemy fighters into an engagement, "Superheat" CAP was duly warned of two MiG-17s (from the 923rd FR) approaching them from below under cloud. As Wyman and Bellinger dived into the undercast with their afterburners ignited in an attempt to locate their quarry, a MiG suddenly appeared directly in front of them. While Bellinger violently maneuvered to avoid a midair collision, Wyman decelerated to avoid overtaking the enemy aircraft. He then saw, to his horror, that the MiG was almost in a firing position behind Tinker, who had overshot the aircraft and then accidentally unplugged his headset, losing radio contact. Wyman yelled an unheard warning to Tinker.

A second 923rd FR MiG-17 then approached Wyman from behind. Tinker saw it and tried to cut the aircraft off, only to lose sight of the jet in a cloud bank. Bellinger and Wyman then tackled a third MiG, and all five aircraft soon went into a spiraling Lufbery Circle tail chase. Wyman was set up for a gun attack at very low altitude, and he managed to get some cannon hits on one MiG's wing before his guns jammed, following up with a Sidewinder miss. The "Superheat" combat report included the comment that "the F-8 had little capability to shoot down the MiGs in this encounter because the cannons were completely unreliable and the MiGs stayed inside [AIM-9] missile minimum range."

Bellinger tried a high yo-yo to attack a MiG, but Ngo Duc Mai crossed the circle in his fighter, moved in behind Bellinger's F-8E, and fired, removing part of its tail, damaging the hydraulics, and weakening the wing. Tinker realized that he had another MiG close behind him and dived to escape. Meanwhile, Wyman fired his last Sidewinder at Tinker's assailant, but it failed to detonate.

Bellinger, escorted by Wyman, headed for Da Nang as his fuel and hydraulic systems began to drain out. He was also unable to take on fuel from a tanker because his hydraulic inflight refueling probe was inoperable. Flying at 225 knots, he hid in clouds where possible. Just short of Da Nang, his fuel ran out and he had to eject over the sea. Wyman followed him down and chased away Vietnamese junks that moved in to capture his boss while they awaited the rescue helicopter. On October 9 that year Bellinger was able to exact his revenge.

The MiG units had their third and final success against F-8s on September 6, 1966 during a transport hub strike near Phu Ly. Nguyen Van Bay, who became the VPAF's top MiG-17 ace with seven victories, led a particularly skillful Gia Lam-based 923rd FR MiG-17 flight including Vo Van Man (credited with five kills), Tran Huyen, and Luu Huy Chao (six victories). They encountered a TARCAP division of VF-111 F-8Es led by Lt Cdr Foster "Tooter" Teague, with USAF exchange pilot Capt Wilfred Abbott leading the second section. Teague took his two F-8Es inshore to cover *Oriskany*-based A-4Es from VA-163 and VA-164, while Abbott and Lt Randy Rime orbited offshore. In due course Abbott's section was called in to relieve Teague's, and they headed over the coast in line astern through cloud, taking up TARCAP station for the A-4s.

Suddenly, on their final orbit at 6,000–7,000ft, they were unexpectedly confronted by Bay and Van Man as they weaved through the clouds. Abbott noticed them seconds before Van Man fired 37mm shells at Rime's Crusader from 1,500ft. A second, corrected 23mm burst at close quarters hit the cockpit and canopy area, injuring Rime with glass splinters. With his fuel tanks holed, canopy split, no radio, and one leading edge flap blown off, Rime dived for safety, recovering with only 300lbs of fuel remaining. He could not raise his wing, and one main landing gear wheel separated during a high-speed arrestment on *Oriskany*.

Abbott had climbed to cover his wingman as soon as he had seen the MiGs, turning at 90 degrees towards them. Despite the latter maneuver presenting

Bay with a difficult deflection angle shot, he repeatedly hit Abbott's jet in the nose and cockpit, shattering the canopy and starting an intense fire. The F-8 pilot was forced to eject, sustaining a broken leg in the process – he was quickly captured. Abbott was VF-111's only loss to an enemy aircraft, although CVW-16 had a total of nine Crusaders destroyed in combat during the cruise.

Bay had already been credited with Lt Eastman's RF-8A on June 21, and he had participated in the loss of Lt Cdr Black's F-8E during that same mission. Luu Huy Chao, in Bay's flight, was typical of many contemporary VPAF pilots. Before training in China, he had never even sat in an aircraft, or a boat for that matter, and he was made aware during his meeting with Ho Chi Minh that his squadron's MiG-17s were older and far less capable than the US fighters he was to engage in combat.

"Blue Bandit"

The Crusader's first MiG-21 ("Blue bandit") kill, and CVW-16's only aerial success during its second war cruise, went to Cdr Dick Bellinger on October 9, 1966. He had led a "Superheat" division escorting 24 A-4s from *Intrepid* on an Alpha strike on a bridge at Phu Ly, 30 miles south of Hanoi. Soon after crossing the coast and setting up an orbit at very low level, shielded by high ground, they heard from a VAW-11 E-1B Tracer radar picket aircraft that MiGs were 40 miles distant.

Bellinger and wingman Lt Lee Prost immediately climbed hard to meet them from their low-altitude patrol station. They saw a MiG-21 approaching an *Iron Hand* A-4E and accelerated to stop its attack, as did the other F-8 TARCAP section. The VPAF pilot in turn spotted the Crusaders, inverted his aircraft and performed a "split-S" maneuver, followed by Bellinger, who stayed with the gyrating MiG, firing an AIM-9B and an AIM-9D from an inverted position as his opponent entered a steep dive. Sidewinders fired in a dive were often distracted by ground heat, but this time one removed the MiG's wing and the second detonated close by. Bellinger pulled out of his steep dive at 200ft, having scored the third MiG-21 kill of the war, and the first for the US Navy.

The VPAF pilot, Nguyen Van Minh, was apparently able to eject before his fighter hit the ground. With fellow MiG-21 pilot Pham Than Ngan, he had claimed a VF-154 F-4B from *Coral Sea*, flown by Lt Cdr Charles Tanner and Lt Ross Terry, earlier in that same Phu Ly mission. Finally, a MiG-17 had been downed by RESCAP flight A-1H Skyraider pilot Lt(jg) Tom Patton from VA-176 while covering a determined, but ultimately unsuccessful, rescue attempt by an SH-3 Sea King crew launched to try and extract Tanner and Terry.

Crusaders next clashed with MiGs in May 1967, when CVW-21's third war

Cdr Dick Bellinger re-enacts his MiG-21 kill for Lt Dick Wyman (facing Bellinger) on October 9, 1966 on the flightdeck of *Oriskany* as pilots from VF-162 walk back to their ready room. Following one of the war's classic dogfights, Wyman would claim his own kill (over a MiG-17) on December 14, 1967 during *Oriskany*'s third war cruise. The Naval Aviators' camouflaged flightsuits were actually "Duck Hunter" civilian wear bought pre-cruise by many CVW-16 pilots from a sporting store near their NAS Lemoore, California, base. (Peter Mersky Collection)

VF-211's Capt Ron Lord (a USAF exchange officer) and Lt Cdr "Mo" Wright point out the location of their dogfight with MiG-17s on May 1, 1967, which resulted in Wright scoring a kill and Lord being credited with having damaged his opponent. Their sweat-stained flightsuits attest to the rigors of the engagement. (US Navy)

cruise (this time embarked in *Bon Homme Richard*) coincided with a peak in VPAF fighter activity. This enabled VF-211 to become, in the squadron historian's words, "the US Navy's leading MiG killers, with six MiGs destroyed and six damaged" in engagements including "the two largest dogfights in naval aviation history." Officially, the score was nine MiGs divided among CVW-21's two Crusader squadrons (VF-24 and VF-211) and Skyhawk unit VA-76.

The first attack on North Vietnam's airfields on May 1 included the notable shoot-down of a MiG-17 by former F-8 pilot Lt Cdr T. R. "Ted" Swartz, who led a flak suppression mission in an A-4C from VA-76. The Skyhawks were escorted by Crusaders from VF-24. VF-211 was also supplying some of the eight escort F-8Es for the *Iron Hand* Skyhawks over Kep that day, and Lt Cdr Marshall "Mo" Wright destroyed a MiG-17 from the North Korean "Doan Z" contingent flying with the 923rd FR. Cdr Paul Speer, commanding VF-211, led the two F-8 divisions, but he and his wingman had to drop out with mechanical problems, leaving only two F-8Es from the unit – the aircraft flown by Lt Cdr "Mo" Wright and USAF exchange officer Capt Ron Lord. They set up a CAP station north of Kep at 12,000ft, while the VF-24 jets mounted their CAP between Kep and Yen Bai.

As Wright's section began their orbit, a MiG call was heard and three silver MiG-17s were detected flying fast at very low altitude at the Crusaders' "two o'clock" position, under the strike formation. Wright and Lord dived in a right turn and achieved a position around 800 yards behind the third MiG-17, flown by Ly Txang Il. In a textbook launch, Wright's AIM-9D flew directly into the MiG's tailpipe, blowing its tail section off. The VPAF fighter pitched down suddenly and its wings separated, leaving the piloted wreck to crash in a ball of fire.

Wright returned to his CAP "perch" as the strike force A-4s began to egress after VA-76 pilot Lt Cdr Jim Rollins damaged a fleeing MiG. Another A-4C pilot with two MiGs on his tail called in the F-8 CAP. Capt Lord (in "Nickel 102") was in a good position, and he damaged the enemy jet's left wing with gunfire as it dived away. He was unable to follow the MiG, however, as the VPAF pilot made an extremely tight left turn in afterburner at around 100ft and flew towards a known AAA concentration, presumably hoping that the F-8s would follow and be hit.

Wright, in "loose deuce" formation, now acquired Lord's MiG and started to set up his missiles as he moved in behind it for a textbook Sidewinder shot. Unfortunately, the missile selector automatically moved to pylon station 2, which held a radar-guided AIM-9C rather than the required AIM-9D on station 3 that Wright assumed would be selected. He stayed behind the MiG, waiting for an IR seeker tone to show it was ready to launch, but nothing

happened as the AIM-9C had no IR seeker. He continued the pursuit as far as he could but eventually had to break off from what would have been a near-certain kill.

May Day

May 19, 1967 was not only Ho Chi Minh's 77th birthday, it was also the Crusader's day, for four MiG-17s were shot down by CVW-21 F-8 pilots during missions that marked the first US Navy strikes on Hanoi. A series of "Doctor Pepper" strikes commenced on that date, with aircraft attacking targets three times daily at fixed hours.

One of the missions flown on the 19th saw A-4E-equipped VA-212 (also assigned to CVW-21) employ AGM-62 Walleye guided bombs – a new weapon that had made its combat debut with this unit two months earlier. VF-211 escorted the Skyhawks on these Walleye drops against Hanoi targets such as the Bac Giang thermal power plant; the first US Navy strike inside the North Vietnamese capital. Twelve F-8Es led by Cdr Paul Speer (flying his 150th mission) accompanied the two Walleye-toting Skyhawks, led by VA-212 CO Cdr Homer Smith, at low altitude through mountainous terrain that included the notorious "Thud Ridge" 20 miles northwest of Hanoi.

VF-24's F-8Cs were also heavily involved in the May 19 engagements, downing two MiGs. Cdr B. C. "Bobby" Lee and his wingman Lt(jg) Kit Smith were flak suppressors, carrying Zunis on three missile stations and a single Sidewinder on the fourth (station 1). The first intervention by 923rd FR MiGs came as they approached the target, Lee spotting a MiG-17 chasing an A-6 Intruder. He alerted squadronmate Lt Phil Wood, who turned towards the MiG and moved into its "eight o'clock" position, closing fast in afterburner. Wood heard a firm "growl" from his Sidewinder as it acquired the target and he fired

F-8E BuNo 150923 was used by Lt Cdr "Mo" Wright to down his MiG-17 on May 1, 1967, at which point it was "Nickel 104." The jet was subsequently assigned to Lt(jg) Tom Hall (who is seen here taxiing towards *Bon Homme Richard*'s bow catapults), who was shot down by AAA for the second time in four days on June 10, 1967 and taken prisoner. BuNo 150923 remained with VF-211 until June 20, 1972, when it was fatally damaged by 37mm AAA during a strafing mission in the Mu Gia Pass. Squadron CO Cdr J. W. "Jimmy" Davis was rescued. (US Navy)

the missile. The deflection angle was excessive and it lost track, but the weapon made the Vietnamese pilot break off from the Intruder. He leveled off and dived for cover in a valley, with Wood close behind, firing two bursts of 20mm and seeing some hits. Conscious that he was supposed to be protecting the A-4 bombers, Wood abandoned the pursuit.

As they approached the very heavily defended target area, the A-4s and their accompanying VF-211 TARCAP Crusaders climbed to begin their attack runs, while VF-24's section engaged the AAA defenses with Zunis and 20mm rounds. A flight of MiG-17s, which had apparently mistaken the F-8s for USAF F-105s, then approached from behind. Surrounded at 2,000ft by bursting AAA and SAMs (30 were fired), Speer turned to follow a 923rd FR MiG-17 that was passing on his left. He and his quarry then entered a series of five high-G "scissors" maneuvers in a shallow dive. Speer attempted a Sidewinder shot but the missile fell away, defeated by the G-forces. The MiG then broke out of the "scissors" with a reverse turn, giving Speer another opportunity. His second AIM-9D detonated close to the MiG's rear fuselage, although it flew on. Speer closed for a 20mm burst, but the MiG was already fatally damaged. The fighter erupted in flames and dived into the ground.

Lt(jg) Joseph Shea, Speer's wingman, noticed Nguyen Huu Diet's unmarked MiG-17 flying parallel to them in pursuit of an A-4, and the CO of VF-211 quickly gave him the lead to attack it. Shea fired 20mm rounds at Diet to make him abandon his attack, the VPAF pilot banking to the left. This maneuver presented Shea with an easier target for his guns and the two Sidewinders he also fired. Both missiles exploded near the MiG, sending it into a rapid descent and fiery crash, from which Diet escaped by ejection. Shea flew through the fireball no more than 200ft above the ground, collecting small-arms damage in the process. The two "Nickel" Crusader pilots then went in search of a KA-3B tanker.

Wood, meanwhile, had returned to the strike force as it began its attacks through fierce flak but lost contact with his wingman, Lt(jg) Bill Metzger, who had seen the MiG-17 previously pursued by his section lead escape. He tried to catch it, but failed to see the results of his missile shot as the MiG disappeared into cloud. As Wood looked around for his wingman, cannon shells began to streak past his canopy and four hit his Crusader's fuselage, forcing debris into the engine. Turning hard, he made the MiG-17 pilot (Nguyen Van Phi) reverse his turn and fly "wings level," making him vulnerable to Wood's second Sidewinder at a range of 2,000ft. Although the missile initially seemed to have lost "lock," it changed course, flew towards the MiG's tail and exploded, cutting off the rear fuselage. Phi ejected, but his parachute failed to open and he was killed.

Having lost his radio, air-conditioning, TACAN, and afterburner as a result of Phi's attack, Wood joined up with Speer's F-8 and was led to a VAH-4 Det L A-3B tanker. Still short of fuel even after rendezvousing with the Skywarrior, he found *Kitty Hawk* and persuaded the landing signals officer to wave off an A-4 that was about to recover so that he could take the wire instead. As Wood advanced his throttle to increase power for landing, the jet's afterburner section exploded. Once safely on deck, his victorious but severely damaged Crusader (BuNo 147029) was suitably daubed with rude slogans – a traditional "punishment" for all who land on the wrong carrier. It was later resurrected as an F-8K.

Shortly after completing his flak suppression attack, Cdr Lee saw a MiG-17 (flown by Tran Minh Phuong) flying parallel with him and his wingman. It then turned in front of them, at which point Lee – formerly an RF-8A pilot – reached down and selected Station 1 on his wafer switch for his single AIM-9D as the MiG turned ahead of him. He fired, lost sight of the missile in the turn but then re-acquired it as the Sidewinder exploded, severing the MiG's rear fuselage and killing the pilot.

Two Crusaders were among the seven US Navy aircraft lost during the May 19 operation, with both pilots becoming PoWs. Lt Cdr Kay Russell in the second VF-211 TARCAP section was hit by the copious AAA that surrounded this high-priority target and then by a yellow-painted SA-2 – one of 32 fired at the Alpha strike. Metzger's jet was hit by heavy AAA just after he had chased Wood's MiG, and he had to eject with severe shrapnel injuries. It was a high price to pay for a failed Walleye attack (the release altitude was too low), but a second strike with AGM-62s the following day caused severe damage to the thermal power plant, although Cdr Homer Smith was shot down by AAA and later died in captivity.

Sixteen MiGs had vectored towards the Alpha strike group on May 19 and the F-8 squadrons had destroyed a quarter of them. It was an unsustainable

MiG MASTER

On May 19, 1967, VF-211 CO Cdr Paul Speer (in F-8E BuNo 150348) led a TARCAP of two Crusaders from his unit and two F-8Cs from VF-24 for the very first Skyhawk AGM-62 Walleye guided-bomb attack on Hanoi's Bac Giang thermal power plant. The strike force was met by extremely heavy AAA and 32 SAMs. Speer also spotted several MiG-17s closing on the Skyhawks and Crusaders from behind.

It was at this point that he and his wingman Lt(jg) Joe Shea (in F-8E BuNo 150661) turned to face the VPAF fighters, with Speer entering into a "scissors" maneuver with MiG-17 2501 of the 923rd FR. Its pilot, Phan Thanh Tai, made a high-G right turn at an altitude of 2,000ft and Speer followed, firing an AIM-9D which did not track correctly. Having hit the MiG with his second Sidewinder, Speer closed to gun range at low altitude, only for the enemy fighter to suddenly start trailing flames from its jet pipe. The aircraft rolled inverted and crashed in a fireball, killing Tai.

loss rate for the VPAF, and MiG activity declined for several weeks, exacerbated by an unauthorized strafing attack on Yen Bai airfield by VF-111's Lt Cdr "Tooter" Teague and Lt Joe Satrapa that destroyed at least two more MiG-17s. However, on July 21, Yen Bai sortied eight MiG-17s to oppose a CVW-21 "mini-Alpha" strike on the Ta Xa petroleum storage area near Haiphong. *Bon Homme Richard's* Crusaders downed three of them and claimed a fourth as a probable in a series of turning fights that pitted the F-8 pilots' skill against the more agile MiG-17 as never before.

Lt Cdr Marion "Red" Isaacks was leading the strike's MiGCAP division with wingman Lt Don McKillip. Four MiG-17s were noticed above them at 9,000ft as the bombing began. Isaacks climbed towards the enemy fighters and quickly acquired a firing solution on one of them. His first Sidewinder appeared to have a good launch "tone," but it did not guide. A second missile refused to launch, so Isaacks tried the third and it flew straight into the MiG's tailpipe, exploding its engine in a huge fireball. Seconds later, Korean War veteran Isaacks saw tracers passing his right wing. "I glanced down to my right and found myself looking down the intake of another MiG." Four rounds hit his right wing-fold area and flaps, causing a small fire. Isaacks pulled hard on the stick and the MiG passed very close beneath him and vanished.

Assigned to fellow MiG killer Lt Cdr Bobby Lee (his kill marking is painted beneath the cockpit), VF-24 F-8C BuNo 146992 was flown by Lt Cdr Bob Kirkwood for his July 21, 1967 MiG-17 victory. The squadron's MiG total, including Lt Phil Dempewolf's "probable", are painted on the aircraft's ventral fin. The Crusader was photographed on the ramp at NAS Miramar in the late summer of 1967 following the completion of CVW-21's highly eventful war cruise. (Terry Panopalis Collection)

Its departure was probably encouraged by the presence of *Iron Hand* A-4 pilot Lt Cdr T. R. Swartz (already a CVW-21 MiG killer), who saw Isaacks' plight and sped after the enemy jet, firing Zuni rockets that distracted the VPAF pilot. Isaacks made an emergency "Mayday" call and squadronmate Lt Cdr Bob Kirkwood joined him. The damaged F-8C (BuNo 147018) remained flyable, and Isaacks was able to cross the beach as the strike force continued its attacks. Over water, the hydraulic fluid fire extinguished, but Isaacks was unsure about the state of his hydraulic system ahead of a landing attempt. With the aid of emergency air bottles to raise his wing, he was able to make a safe carrier recovery.

Kirkwood's own victory that day, as "Page Boy" section leader, was the F-8's second, and final, "guns only" kill, Lt Gene Chancy's (on July 21, 1966) being the first. He launched a Sidewinder at one of the eight MiG-17s that tangled with them but it lacked a good acquisition tone and went ballistic. He then fired a second at the MiG that Isaacks was engaging, but the latter pilot's missile reached the target first. He then went after "Doan Z" pilot Ly Dong Su, firing his final AIM-9. It exploded close to the VPAF fighter without causing visible damage. Resorting to his guns, Kirkwood followed the MiG as it turned gently and fired at around 600ft, closing to just 300ft. His tracking was accurate and many of his rounds hit Su's aircraft, causing a major conflagration in the fuselage. Su ejected but did not survive.

1600 hrs, December 14, 1967

CANAL DES BAMBOUS

1 VF-162's Lt Richard E. Wyman ("Superheat 204") leads an F-8 TARCAP from *Oriskany* charged with escorting A-4s mining the Canal des Bambous (Canal of Bamboo) near Haiphong. Cdr "Cal" Swanson ("Superheat 201"), who was the Crusader formation's original leader, passes the lead to Wyman when his radio fails. This is VF-162's first dedicated fighter mission for some time after numerous ground attack sorties.

2 Whilst flying at 15,000ft and 450 knots, Wyman detects a distant MiG-21 on radar but it turns away. Shortly thereafter, *Iron Hand* A-4 pilot Lt Chuck Nelson from VA-164, who is flying ahead of the Crusaders, reports that he has spotted a lone, camouflaged MiG-17 five miles ahead of him at low altitude.

3 Nelson begins weaving and turning behind the MiG to prevent the jet from getting away from the closing F-8s.

4 The MiG pilot spots Wyman and turns sharply towards him. They pass head-on, both firing at each other. Wyman pulls up into a high "yo-yo" roll and turn, before descending in an attempt to get behind the MiG. The latter then turns sharply left and Swanson enters the fight, trying to shoot at the enemy fighter. Its pilot, Nguyen Dinh Phuc, initially attempts to get behind Swanson, before reversing his turn in Wyman's direction. They meet head-on again, and "Superheat 204" makes another high "yo-yo," moving away from Swanson.

5 Wyman and his opponent make two turns, attempting to get behind each other. Wyman again performs high "yo-yo" maneuvers to try and gain the advantage.

6 During one turn Cdr Bob Rasmussen (CO of VF-111) from the second *Iron Hand* escort section slots into the action behind Wyman and fires a Sidewinder that almost hits "Superheat 204" and misses the MiG.

7 Wyman stays behind the MiG through another series of turns, overshooting it on three occasions when his opponent makes a particularly tight turn.

8 Phuc starts a rolling turn to meet Wyman head-on, but when he loses sight of the F-8 he goes wings level on a straight-ahead course. Seizing his opportunity for a clear shot with a missile, Wyman fires a Sidewinder and hits the MiG, which is flying just 50ft above the ground. The jet enters a violent roll as its engine explodes, sending the MiG cartwheeling into a rice paddy.

9 Wyman, with only 2,500lbs of fuel remaining, quickly meets up with Swanson and they head for *Oriskany*.

FOLLOWING PAGES

Lt Cdr "Tim" Hubbard of VF-211 was a highly capable, aggressive aviator who was also a very colorful character out of the cockpit. He claimed a MiG-17 destroyed on July 21, 1967. (US Navy)

To his great surprise, when he joined up with Isaacks to egress, Kirkwood learned that his own F-8C had also been severely damaged. One of the missiles that had zoomed past his aircraft (and which he had assumed were fired by his wingman) had hit his tail without exploding. It had impacted the trailing edge of the right horizontal stabilizer, cut it cleanly off, and proceeded along the fuselage, leaving scratches and probably knocking a Sidewinder off its rail. Kirkwood had been unaware of this happening.

The third MiG downed on July 21 was credited to Lt Cdr Ray "Tim" Hubbard of VF-211. A former VF-51 pilot who had flown F-8s since 1957, he had damaged a MiG with Zuni rockets on April 25, 1967. Hubbard was in the "Pouncer" *Iron Hand* escort for a Shrike missile-carrying Skyhawk flown by Lt Cdr T. R. Swartz four miles ahead of the strike group. Their job was to lure SAM radars into revealing themselves by switching on and emitting signals for the Shrike to home on to. Hubbard's aircraft carried six Zunis and a single AIM-9D.

As they orbited over the target, eight MiG-17s were seen heading into the A-4 strike group. Hubbard assumed the lead and accelerated in afterburner towards the first section of MiGs. He closed in behind the silver No. 2 aircraft, but was too close for an AIM-9D shot as the MiGs began a tight left turn towards him. Hubbard's gunnery skills were known to be superior, and allowing for a greater deflection angle, he opened fire and saw multiple strikes on the wings and fuselage of a "Doan Z"-piloted MiG wings and fuselage. Meanwhile, as previously noted, Swartz saw two MiG-17s threatening "Red" Isaacks' Crusader and he went after them. Lacking Sidewinder capability, he fired Zunis at them and missed, but drove the MiGs away nonetheless.

When a stream of blazing 37mm "tennis balls," leaving green tracer smoke, flew past Hubbard, he threw his Crusader into a high-G barrel roll to make his pursuers – another MiG-17 section – overshoot. Again, he was able to move in behind the second MiG and inflict serious damage with his guns. His other weapons were an AIM-9D, which had failed its pre-launch serviceability test and went ballistic when fired, and his Zunis. The two fighters increased their turning rate so much that the first two Zunis missed. Allowing more deflection, Hubbard fired two more pairs of Zunis and one exploded near the wing of Ly Do In's MiG, which began a series of abrupt turns and counter-turns while decelerating. Hubbard executed another high-G barrel roll to avoid over-shooting the MiG and followed up with 20mm rounds until he ran out of shells. Pulling his F-8 into another barrel roll, he ended up canopy-to-canopy with the MiG, and eventually saw the pilot eject.

There was also a "probable" MiG kill during the July 21 clash, credited to Kirkwood's wingman, Lt(jg) Phil Dempewolf ("Page Boy 448"). When Kirkwood joined up with Isaacks' damaged F-8 to reach safety, Dempewolf stayed near the target to repel more MiGs. While Kirkwood had gone in pursuit of his first MiG target, Dempewolf checked for another MiG section behind them. Two did appear, turning in to attack him. He made a climbing turn to the left and fired an AIM-9D as the pair also climbed, wings level, northwards. The missile failed to guide, so he accelerated to closer quarters and fired again. Dempewolf's second Sidewinder exploded between the MiGs, making them commit to a diving turn to the right. He closed again and fired his third AIM-9D, but it went ballistic, probably because it was fired with the target against a land background.

Dempewolf then decided to abandon the pursuit, as he knew his fourth Sidewinder had displayed a pre-mission fault. Just then, another MiG-17 appeared ahead of him. He selected the suspect Sidewinder and saw it guiding

1600 hrs, JUNE 26, 1968

NEAR VINH SON

1 Cdr Lowell "Moose" Myers ("Batter Up 116"), CO of VF-51, is flying a BARCAP with Lts John Quisenberry and Bert Harden, the trio of F-8Hs being controlled by USS *Jouett* (DLG-29). Myers takes the formation down to treetop level, crossing the beach at 600 knots. They are intercepted shortly thereafter by two MiG-17s and two MiG-21s.

2 The MiG-21s, with the leader one mile ahead of his wingman, together with the MiG-17s a further two miles behind, pass above the F-8s at an altitude of about 7,000ft. Myers positions the Crusaders slightly to the left of the oncoming MiGs, which have been sighted at his "ten o'clock" position 20 degrees left of his nose. The MiG-17s are seen to break off the interception at this point and head back north.

3 Myers tells Harden to climb and tackle the second (trailing) MiG-21 while he climbs steeply to attack the leader, taking advantage of the "Blue bandit's" poor rearward and downward visibility.

4 As Myers banks in a climbing turn in order to get behind the MiG-21, its pilot sees a reflection off the F-8's wing. He turns towards "Batter Up 116," who pulls his jet into an almost vertical climb and they pass head-on before entering ascending turns.

5 The MiG-21 commences a right ascending turn, which Myers matches from above his foe. He tries to point the nose of the F-8 down in the direction of his target, firing at the MiG as he passes 300ft behind the jet. Myers misses.

6 Myers completes two 180-degree turns as he tries to get on the tail of the MiG-21, losing speed as he does so. The enemy pilot then turns back towards the F-8, and the two fighters cross over each other again. Myers matches his opponent's turn with a "scissors" maneuver, firing at the MiG each time it passes within a 30-degree "cone" 2,500ft ahead of him. With each of the three "scissors" turns he completes, Myers gradually gains ground on the VPAF fighter.

7 The MiG pilot commences a 70-degree climb in afterburner to escape, presenting an excellent Sidewinder target. Myers pulls in behind him at 3,000ft and fires three missiles. The first two "cut the plane in half," giving Myers the distinction of claiming VF-51's first MiG kill.

8 Myers launches his last remaining Sidewinder at the departing wingman, but the weapon is fired "hopelessly out of range" and fails to home correctly. The MiG escapes in a 70-degree climb. The Crusaders regroup and return to *Bon Homme Richard*.

FOLLOWING PAGES

straight towards the MiG. He never saw the result, for two more MiGs appeared to his right, heading straight for him. Dempewolf attempted to engage them as they dived below him, but the deflection angle was too great and his bullets passed well behind them. Returning to the site of his final missile attack, he saw a pilot descending beneath a square VPAF parachute. This was also seen by some A-4 pilots, but there was no eye-witness evidence to confirm an aircraft kill.

Five months would pass before the next clash between Crusaders and MiGs. Lt Richard Wyman of VF-162, embarked in *Oriskany*, had primarily been involved in ground attack missions for the first five months of CVW-16's third war cruise. However, on December 14, 1967, he flew as "Superheat 204" with his CO, Cdr "Cal" Swanson, as fighter escorts for an Alpha strike on a bridge near Haiphong harbor. Three of the five assigned F-8s had become unserviceable, leaving Swanson and Wyman as the VF-162 TARCAP section. Approaching the target, amid many MiG warnings, Wyman took over the lead when Swanson's radar failed.

Four MiG-17s and a MiG-21 were reported by *Red Crown*, with the latter fighter used as bait to lure the escort Crusaders away. Wyman briefly chased the MiG-21, but he then heard that the *Iron Hand* VA-164 A-4E (flown by Lt Chuck Nelson) and its escort F-8, flown by Lt Cdr Dick Schaffert (see Chapter 1), were under attack by MiG-17s. A VF-111 F-8C flown by former *Blue Angel* pilot and squadron CO Cdr Bob Rasmussen, escorting a "pouncer" *Iron Hand* A-4E flown by Lt Dennis Weichmann, engaged the MiG. Weichmann fired 40 rounds, despite his Skyhawk still being loaded with Shrikes and bombs.

Wyman, speeding at 500 knots to reach the action, used his radar to pick up both the A-4 and the MiG-17 ahead of him at 15,000ft. A sustained duel with expert MiG-17 pilot Nguyen Dinh Phuc ensued in which the VPAF combat veteran impressed the F-8 pilots, although he lost his life when his jet was struck by the final low-altitude AIM-9D launched by Wyman.

Lt Cdr John B. Nichols (right) of VF-191 is congratulated by his CO, Cdr C. H. Tuomela, after his July 9, 1968 MiG-17 kill. Nichols later commanded VF-24, and he was one of just five pilots to log more than 3,000 hours in Crusaders. (US Navy)

1968

Following six months of little aerial action, Crusaders flying from *Bon Homme Richard* as part of CVW-5 scored three more MiG victories in the summer of 1968. On many occasions during that year MiGs approached F-8 formations, but as VF-24 (embarked in *Hancock*) reported, they "always fled to their sanctuary before contact could be made." However, an afternoon strike on June 26 included a VF-51 division led by veteran Crusader pilot Cdr Lowell R. "Moose" Myers with three "Batter Up" F-8Hs, as one had aborted. Their fleeting 45-second engagement with VPAF fighters resulted in a MiG kill for Myers, who, upon returning to *Bon Homme Richard*, was allowed a "victory" flypast. His victory meant VF-51 had become the first US Navy squadron to down enemy aircraft in World War II (then designated VF-5), Korea, and Vietnam.

Ticonderoga commenced its fourth war cruise in January 1968. Fighters flying from the carrier had not scored any MiG victories on previous deployments, although 25 aircraft had been lost in combat. A "payback" opportunity came on July 9 when Lt Cdr John B. Nichols of VF-191 destroyed a MiG-17 during an RF-8G photo escort mission for Lt Bill Kocar in "Corktip 602." Like Nichols, Kocar was a highly respected F-8 pilot who had been flying Crusaders for more than ten years.

This division of F-8Es from VF-191 includes Lt Cdr John B. Nichols' BuNo 150926 (top), which was marked with the Modex "101" at the time of his MiG victory on July 9, 1968. He used both an AIM-9D and 20mm cannon shells to down his opponent. The aircraft was upgraded into an F-8J in 1968 and lost on May 21, 1969 when it crashed into the Gulf of Tonkin following engine failure. The fighter was assigned to VF-194, embarked in *Oriskany*, at the time. (US Navy)

Nichols had been assigned a BARCAP that day, but Kocar's original escort pilot had suffered ECM equipment failure in his jet, so he swapped places with Nichols just before the latter reached his CAP station. The photo mission continued at around 450 knots and 2,500ft, with Kocar looking for his ten assigned photo targets and Nichols, as "Feedbag 101" in F-8E BuNo 150926, flying 1,500ft above him.

There were no *Red Crown* warnings of MiGs, and jamming by US Navy ECM aircraft had been delayed, although they did manage to jam VHF communications between Nguyen Phi Hung (one of the most experienced pilots in the 923rd FR with five victories) and his GCI. Nichols detected Hung's green-camouflaged MiG-17 approaching fast from behind, and he warned Kocar, who immediately dived and turned 90 degrees towards the coast. Nichols also entered a 5g diving turn, heading in the direction of the MiG. Ignoring tracer rounds that were passing behind him, he continued to turn tightly in order to achieve a good Sidewinder shot at his quarry.

Nichols' first AIM-9D, fired outside parameters, detonated near the sharply turning MiG-17 without inflicting any damage, but Hung, lacking GCI guidance, made the fatal mistake of reversing his turn and lighting his afterburner, presenting an ideal target for the second Sidewinder. The missile exploded inside the MiG's rear section and the fighter slowed down as its engine stopped.

Avoiding a severe overshoot, Nichols switched to "guns" as the MiG continued with a right turn. At a range of 500ft he saw around ten strikes on its uppersurfaces. A wing then detached, followed by further structural failure and debris, which Nichols had to fly through. The VPAF fighter dived into the ground with Hung still aboard only one minute after Nichols had first spotted him. The second MiG-17, which Nichols guessed was the source of the tracers, although he never saw it, had vanished. When the two pilots returned to the carrier, they performed a spectacular victory flypast at 650 knots, followed by a zoom climb to 40,000ft.

Final Victories

President Lyndon Johnson's 1968 bombing halt severely restricted US Navy activity north of the 19th parallel, while allowing the North Vietnamese forces time to recover and massively increase their assets. Carrier missions were confined to armed reconnaissance and interdiction of communications and logistics south of that line, with up to eight aircraft launches daily. MiGs remained a threat, however,

F-8E BuNo 150349 was used by VF-53 executive officer Lt Cdr Guy Cane to claim his MiG-17 on July 29, 1968 after he and Lt(jg) Dexter Manlove became involved in what Cane described as "a real old-fashioned dogfight" near Vinh. (US Navy)

including those based at a new forward staging airfield at Bai Thuong near the 19th parallel.

In 1968, US Navy fighters shot down six MiGs, and five of them fell to Crusader pilots. It was an outcome that reflected their success in the preceding three years of the war in which they had scored 14 of the US Navy's total of 29 MiG kills.

VF-53's first MiG victory took place on July 29, 1968. Leading a MiGCAP, Lt Cdr Guy Cane and his wingman, Lt(jg) Dexter Manlove, were joined by Lt Cdr Sandy Button and Lt(jg) Chuck Conrad in the TARCAP F-8E section. Near the coast, they were warned of up to eight MiGs approaching from the north, and they dropped to 200ft as they went "feet dry." CVW-5's operational report recorded:

> In spite of heavy concentrations of AAA and automatic weapons in the area, the division of F-8s crossed the beach at extremely low altitude and 630 knots. The flight had penetrated about seven miles inland when two MiG-17s were sighted [by Manlove] at 10 o'clock high at 2–3 miles heading at about 400 knots. The two opposing sections of airplanes met almost head-on and turned towards one another. At this time [Conrad in the] second section of F-8s sighted two more MiG-17s descending from a cloud to the west, and they turned to engage them. Thereafter, the entire fight took place in the same 2–3 miles diameter airspace between the surface and an altitude of about 6,000ft.
>
> After his initial turn, Cdr Cane executed a maximum performance port reversal into the bandits, which placed him directly aft of the leader after only one turn. An AIM-9D was fired "in envelope" on a good tone and it appeared to guide initially. However, the missile missed as the MiG leader increased his rate of turn. Executing another hard port reversal, Cdr Cane maneuvered to a position behind the lead wingman and fired his second missile, which guided well. "It detonated just short of his tailpipe," Cane reported. "I thought I had missed until a chunk of his starboard wing came off and the MiG went into a nose-dive, spiraling." Cdr Cane and his wingman, Lt(jg) Manlove, observed a huge fireball on the ground directly below them where the MiG impacted. Reversing again into the fight, a "guns" attack was then pressed on a third MiG to a range of 200ft, but no hits were observed.

The dogfight continued for five minutes of "intense close-in fighting. Cdr Cane's division, providing magnificent mutual support, achieved the tactical advantage initially and never relinquished it throughout the fight." With all their fuel and ordnance at critical levels, Cane then had to withdraw "Firefighter division," leaving the blazing wreck of Le Si Diep's MiG on the ground.

With Cane and Button engaging two MiG flights, this confrontation had split into two separate fights that could have yielded other successes. Manlove had a "sitting duck" MiG in his sights at one point, but his AIM-9 would not fire and his guns jammed. Both Button and Conrad fired AIM-9Ds that seemed to guide but lost their lock and fell away. Conrad's guns jammed as well.

August 1, 1968 brought CVW-5's first MiG-21 kill. The carrier air wing's VF-51 was in the process of undertaking its only deployment with rebuilt F-8Hs, while sister-squadron VF-53 was still equipped with appreciably newer F-8Es. On the 1st, Lt Norm McCoy was flying F-8H BuNo 147916 on a photo escort sortie near Vinh, the carrier also launching a VF-53 section a little later to cover a strike at Vinh Son – only the leader, Lt George Hise, was able to take off, however. When the photo run was completed, McCoy was diverted to the A-4 strike force to join Hise and form an escort section.

As the Skyhawks commenced their attack, *Red Crown* reported MiG-17s moving towards them. Upon hearing this, the A-4 pilots immediately dropped their ordnance and headed back over the coast, leaving the two Crusaders ("Viking" flight) to seek out the MiGs. They flew north at 450mph and 9,000ft, separated by more than a mile in "combat spread" in order to watch for threats to each other's aircraft. They saw nothing and turned back in the direction of the coast.

At the same time, two VF-111 Det 11 F-8Cs from *Intrepid* led by Lt Tony Nargi had entered the area, looking for the same MiGs. As the two F-8 sections closed on each other, a MiG-21 appeared, commencing an attack from above and behind Hise's position. McCoy called a warning and Hise broke away sharply just as the MiG pilot, Nguyen Hong Nhi, fired an "Atoll" missile at him. Hise noticed a "dart-like form" at the periphery of his vision. The weapon missed and the MiG dived away at high speed towards home, followed by his wingman. "I knew we were fat then," McCoy reported, "because the MiG turned to the right and we were both in a position to chase him."

"Viking" section duly set off in pursuit, and McCoy got a good Sidewinder tone on the leader's engine exhaust as the MiG began a right turn. The missile, one of his four, lost track and Hise took over. His AIM-9D flew past the MiG without fusing correctly, as did his second, which was distracted by cloud. They then flew through the cloud and detected the MiG-21 flying very low ahead of them.

F-8 pilots claimed five victories in 1968, with three of the kills being credited to Naval Aviators from VF-51 and VF-53 embarked in *Bon Homme Richard*. VF-51's Cdr "Moose" Myers (who claimed a MiG-21 on June 26) shakes hands with squadronmate Lt Norm McCoy, while Lt George Hise is congratulated by Lt Cdr Guy Cane (both men were from VF-53). This photograph was taken shortly after Hise and McCoy had recovered back on board their carrier after dueling with two MiG-21s on August 1. McCoy downed one "Blue bandit" and Hise damaged the other. Cane's MiG-17 kill had been scored three days previously on July 29. (Peter Mersky Collection)

VF-111 Det 11's Lt Tony Nargi and Lt(jg) Alex Rucker are photographed with *Intrepid's* executive officer, Cdr T. D. Brown, immediately after returning from their successful MiG-21 engagement on September 1, 1968. This was the carrier's second, and last, aerial victory of the Vietnam War. It was also the last conventional kill for the F-8 Crusader. (US Navy)

At that point, the famously assertive Nargi, who allegedly pursued MiGs beyond the Chinese border illegally, arrived and joined the chase, cutting in front of McCoy just as the latter was about to release a Sidewinder. McCoy and the MiG entered a hard right turn, throwing Nargi's jet out to the left, and McCoy got his missile shot but it failed to guide. He accelerated even closer to Nguyen Hong Nhi and fired a third AIM-9D within a mile of the target and in a shallower turn that allowed the missile to explode alongside the MiG's center fuselage. A large fireball appeared and the MiG dived into the jungle, its pilot having ejected seconds earlier.

Tony Nargi had to wait more than a month for his next MiG opportunity. Flying as "Old Nick 103" on September 19 on his 111th mission, he claimed the F-8's last conventional MiG kill of the war. That day, Nargi and Lt(jg) Alex Rucker were a VF-111 TARCAP section for an Alpha strike, working with a "Nickel" section from VF-211 (embarked in *Hancock*) led by Lt Pat Scott. Their *Red Crown* controller on board USS *Long Beach* (CGN-9) soon vectored them towards a pair of MiG-21s approaching from the northeast, with a second flight closing from the northwest. The two TARCAP sections united under Scott to meet the MiGs, although his jet was so afflicted by problems with its radio and compass that Nargi effectively called the shots.

He soon saw a MiG-21 above them, called "Tally ho!" over the radio to announce he was engaging the VPAF fighter and climbed towards it with Rucker, leaving "Nickel" section behind – there was not time to deal with their radio problems and guide them too. The VF-111 section followed the MiG up in a high looping maneuver that allowed Vu Dinh Rang to exploit his fighter's weight advantage and pull well ahead of the Crusaders. However, as the jet descended, Nargi took advantage of the MiG pilot's reverse turn, which took him across the F-8's missile launch envelope. Rang leveled out, probably unable to see the Crusaders, and Nargi was presented with a textbook Sidewinder launch opportunity at less than 2,000ft range. His missile flew into the MiG's jet-pipe, blowing off the entire rear fuselage as Rang ejected.

Rucker, true to his "loose deuce" training, immediately checked their "six o'clock" and spotted the second MiG-21 close behind him, firing an "Atoll" at his F-8. He called to all "Nickel" pilots to break right, and the missile passed by. Nargi performed a barrel roll to make the MiG overshoot, before firing his second AIM-9D, which missed. "Nickel 02" (Lt Leon Swaim) then closed to within 1,500ft of the MiG's tail and took a Sidewinder shot. At the last moment, his quarry saw the weapon and abruptly pulled up, letting it pass. Rucker then fired a missile at it, but the Sidewinder exploded at its maximum range of around two miles, short of the MiG. The final shot came from Scott, who caught the jet in a turn in afterburner. His missile homed on the MiG but failed to explode. Having survived four Sidewinder attacks, the VPAF pilot finally escaped into cloud.

Last "Victory"

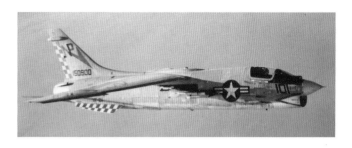

The very last Crusader MiG kill, after a gap of three years and nine months, was achieved by Lt Jerry Tucker of VF-211 (flying from *Hancock*) in F-8J BuNo 150900, although it was not registered as a victory at the time. By that stage in the war, the last four US Navy Crusader squadrons still operating with Seventh Fleet (VF-24, VF-191, VF-194, and VF-211) had been relegated to flying CAP and escort missions that were unlikely to encounter MiGs.

On a May 23, 1972 TARCAP with Lt Cdr Frank Bachman, Tucker took over an intercept from a pair of VF-161 F-4s who had lost the single MiG-17 that they were chasing. He saw the distant sunlight reflection off a MiG's windscreen as the jet flew close to the ground, and turned to get behind it and open fire. It was a mark of the Crusader's persistently fearsome reputation that even in the last year of the US Navy's direct involvement in the Vietnam War, the MiG pilot chose to pitch down and eject before Tucker could launch his AIM-9D. His kill was disallowed on the grounds that it had been achieved without the use of any weapons, despite five USAF pilots being awarded victories in similar circumstances. No more MiGs rose to challenge F-8 CAPs before the cessation of all US air strikes on North Vietnam on January 15, 1973.

F-8 pilots officially had shot down 18 MiGs and claimed two probables by September 1968 for the loss of three Crusaders in aerial combat, giving the aircraft a 6-to-1 kill ratio. F-4B/J pilots achieved a 5.42-to-1 kill ratio over the entire war. Thirteen Phantom II victories were scored by US Navy units in 1965–68 during *Rolling Thunder*, and a further 26 had been added by the time the final MiG was downed by VF-161 on January 12, 1973.

The US Navy lost 116 F-8s and 31 RF-8s, although only three were claimed by MiGs – always in conditions that favored the VPAF, usually enabling pilots to "jump" the Crusaders in poor weather conditions. Eleven were victims of SA-2 sites during CAP missions (six losses) or on flak suppression, *Iron Hand*, or escort sorties. The majority of the rest were shot down by various types of anti-aircraft fire. The US Marine Corps losses comprised 22 F-8s and one RF-8.

Although SAMs were only responsible for a small proportion of the losses, they were a constant threat, mainly in forcing US Navy aircraft down to lower altitudes where they became more vulnerable to AAA. The exactly timed barrel roll maneuver, or diving turn, required to dodge a SAM also caused a loss of altitude and was not always sufficient to break the missile's lock. For example, on October 26, 1967, VF-162's Lt(jg) Charles Rice, who was undertaking a flak suppression mission for an Alpha strike on the Bac Giang thermal power plant, threw his bomb-laden F-8E into a violent climbing roll to avoid an oncoming SA-2, but it found him and blew the wing off his fighter – Rice ejected and he was captured.

On occasion, there was not time to attempt an evasion maneuver. On January 4, 1968, Rice's squadronmate Lt(jg) Richard Minnich was killed when a SAM struck his TARCAP F-8E without warning following a strike on the road bridge at Hai Duong. Nevertheless, the real threat to Crusader pilots was AAA.

VF-211 F-8J BuNo 150900 was used by Lt Jerry Tucker on his May 23, 1972 "MiG scaring" mission. In what proved to be the Crusader's final clash with an enemy fighter, the lone VPAF pilot ejected when he saw that Tucker and wingman Lt Cdr Frank Bachman had a firing solution on his MiG-17. The jet is seen here on a CAP mission in 1972 armed with two AIM-9s and bearing the "101" modex of Cdr Jim Davis (VF-211's CO) on its nose. (US Navy)

AFTERMATH

The performance of the F-8 in Vietnam was both surprising and instructive for US Navy planners in many ways. Although pilots took great pride in flying the "last of the gunfighters," their primary weapon when engaging VPAF MiGs was the AIM-9 Sidewinder. Indeed, the fighter's four Mk 12 20mm cannon were usually only employed as a weapon of last resort – they played a significant role in three kills, in combination with AIM-9Ds (Kirkwood and Nichols) or, in one case (Hubbard), in conjunction with an unguided Zuni rocket. The AIM-9D variant was the most used in all cases, although Cdr Bellinger combined one with an AIM-9B for his victory. However, the presence of guns, and the pilots' extensive training in their use, allowed Naval Aviators to place their Crusaders in favorable positions for both gun and Sidewinder engagements.

The Colt-Browning Mk 12s were often unreliable, and it is difficult to estimate the Crusader's likely success in combat over North Vietnam if pilots had had to rely exclusively on them. At any rate, the overall value of a close-in weapon influenced the revival of the cannon for the next generation of naval fighters.

Crusader pilots officially scored 18 MiG-17 and MiG-21 victories for the loss of only three of their own number to enemy fighters. This unequaled Vietnam War record was powerful evidence that there was still a need for a dedicated air superiority fighter. The development of the F-14 and the USAF's F-15 Eagle reflected that realization.

In the 1960s, US Secretary of Defense Robert S. McNamara and his advisors favored multi-purpose types like the F-111 and F-4 Phantom II. The latter acquitted itself well as a fighter, achieving three-quarters of the shootdowns of 198 MiGs throughout the war at an "exchange rate" of 2.8-to-1. However, its all-weather interceptor design origins gave it less maneuverability than the F-8, and it took the establishment of Topgun to give Phantom II pilots the skills to tackle MiGs in close combat. By then, the Crusader had already given way to the F-4 in many US Navy squadrons after a period of unprecedented, confirmed successes in aerial combat that lasted for little more than two years, from June 1966 to September 1968. F-8 pilots already had those dogfighting skills, having worked on air-to-air techniques as part of their primary "day fighter" role since the aircraft's fleet introduction in 1958.

Although Crusaders gave useful service as ground attackers with the US Marine Corps and as flak suppressors within naval Alpha strike packages, they will be remembered as both "hot-rod," double-sonic gunfighters and demanding "steeds" for their pilots to master. Set against their aerial successes was a regrettable record of accidents in operations aboard the relatively small Essex-class carriers they were consigned to from the early 1960s, and of unforgiving handling characteristics when flown by unwary pilots. Despite this, the F-8's reputation as the "last gunfighter" or "MiG master" looks set to remain unequaled.

SELECTED SOURCES

Books

Drendel, Lou, … *And Kill MiGs* (Squadron Signal Publications, 1997)

Francillon, René J., *Tonkin Gulf Yacht Club* (AeroSphere Research Edn., 2018)

Gillchrist, Paul T., *Crusader – Last of the Gunfighters* (Schiffer Military History, 1995)

Ginter, Steve, *F-8 Crusader Navy Fighter Squadrons, Naval Fighters No. 19* (Ginter, 1990)

Grant, Zalin, *Over the Beach – the Air War in Vietnam* (W. W. Norton and Co., 1986)

Gundlach, Louis S., *The Last Gunfighter – F-8 Crusader over North Vietnam* (Hush-Kit, 2020)

Hobson, Chris, *Vietnam Air Losses* (Midland Publishing, 2001)

Kinsey, Bert and Roszak, Rock, *F-8 & RF-8 Crusader* (Detail & Scale Publications, 2019)

McCarthy, Donald J., *MiG Killers – US Air Victories 1965–73* (Specialty Press, 2009)

Mersky, Peter, *Vought F-8 Crusader* (Osprey Publishing, 1989)

Mersky, Peter, *Osprey Duel 61 – F-8 Crusader vs MiG-17* (Osprey Publishing, 2014)

Mersky, Peter, *Osprey Combat Aircraft 7 – F-8 Crusader Units of the Vietnam War* (Osprey Publishing, 1998)

O'Connor, Michael, *MiG Killers of Yankee Station* (New Past Press, Inc., 2003)

Spidle, William D., *Vought F-8 Crusader* (Specialty Press, 2017)

Tillman, Barrett, *MiG Master – Story of the F-8 Crusader* (Nautical and Aviation Publishing, 1980)

Tillman, Barrett and van der Lugt, Henk, *Osprey Aviation Elite Units 36 – VF-11/111 Sundowners* (Osprey Publishing, 2010)

Thomason, Tommy H., *US Naval Air Superiority* (Specialty Press, 2007)

Toperczer, István, *Silver Swallows and Blue Bandits* (Artipresse, 2015)

Weaver, Michael, *An Examination of the F-8 Crusader through Archival Sources* (Air Command and Staff College, 2018)

Wilcox, Robert K., *Scream of Eagles – the Creation of Top Gun* (John Wiley and Sons, Inc., 1990)

Documents

NAVAIR 01-45HHA-TT. F-8 Tactical Manual (Chief of Naval Operations, 1967)

NAVAIR 01-45HHD-1. F-8D and F-8E Flight Manual (Chief of Naval Operations, 1964)

INDEX

Note: page locators in **bold** refer to illustrations, captions and plates.